THE BIBLE YEAR

The Bible Year:
A Journey Through
Scripture in 365 Days

Book

978-1-7910-2341-6 *Paperback*

978-1-7910-2342-3 *ePub*

Leader Guide

978-1-7910-2343-0 *Paperback*

978-1-7910-2344-7 *ePub*

Pastor Guide

978-1-7910-2345-4 *Paperback*

978-1-7910-2346-1 *ePub*

Also by Magrey R. deVega

Awaiting the Already

Embracing the Uncertain

Almost Christmas

Hope for Hard Times

Savior

THE
BIBLE
YEAR

*A Journey Through
Scripture in 365 Days*

MAGREY R. DEVEGA

Abingdon Press | Nashville

The Bible Year

A Journey Through Scripture in 365 Days

Library of Congress Control Number: 2021942079
978-1-7910-2341-6

21 22 23 24 25 26 27 28 29 30 — 10 9 8 7 6 5 4 3 2 1
MANUFACTURED IN THE UNITED STATES OF AMERICA

CONTENTS

INTRODUCTION

Growing up, I heard many metaphors for how to relate to the Bible, helping me connect its strange words and antiquated imagery to ordinary experience. I was told, for example, that the Bible is like a road map: just figure out how to read it, and you'll see the path to your best life. Someone also told me it was a kind of how-to manual: follow its instructions, and your life will be a success. Or consider it like a cookbook, and you'll have the ingredients to a good life.

Those metaphors were all well and good. For a while.

Over time I realized that such images of the Bible, when taken too far, can become much too self-serving. They can lead to a strictly utilitarian view of how the Bible can become useful to us, rather than the more important question: How can we become more faithful in service to God? In *Eat this Book: A Conversation in the Art of Spiritual Reading* (Eerdmans, 2006), Eugene Peterson writes:

> "The most important question we ask of this text is not, 'What does this mean?' but 'What can I obey?' A simple act of obedience will open up our lives to this text far more quickly than any number of Bible studies and dictionaries and concordances" (71).

To reorient our approach to the Scriptures, to make it less about using the Bible and more about becoming useful in God's service, requires one key ingredient: listening.

To grow in our faith, prayer and Scripture reading must go hand in hand. We must read the Bible prayerfully, and we must engage in prayer biblically. "Faith comes from listening," Paul writes to the church in Rome, "but it's listening by means of Christ's message" (Romans 10:17). The text is illumined by prayer; prayer is grounded in text. It is logos and pneuma, word and spirit, united.

That is the value of a sustained encounter with Scripture, a daily practice of reading it and meditating on it. That is our task as we read through the Scriptures together over the days ahead. Not to just read the words in its pages, but to do so prayerfully and responsively. To narrow the sixteen-inch distance between our heads and our hearts and to allow the words of Scripture to shape our thoughts, our emotions, and our behaviors.

Each day, I offer an insight into some portion of the reading, something I find compelling or provocative. You will likely discover other dimensions of the text that catch your attention. But the most important part of this devotional may be the blank space in between the readings, where you are invited to record your own response to Scripture. In this space, take time to consider:

> "What is God revealing to me today, and how will I apply it
> to my life?"

Fill that blank space with what you are hearing from God, and determine ways to commit yourself in obedience to the way and will of God.

Periodically, you will also find short overviews of the readings ahead. Think of these as navigational aids, something to help you get your bearings in Scripture, see where you are and where the next leg of the journey will take you.

May this devotional be much more than a road map for your journey ahead. May it become a living record of your spiritual journey, as the words of the Bible lead you to greater faithfulness and deeper devotion to Jesus Christ.

Welcome to the journey!

—Magrey de Vega

PART 1

THE OLD TESTAMENT
Genesis–Malachi

Genesis 1:1–11:32

When we read the Book of Genesis—and the whole Bible, really—it is far too easy to get caught up in the mechanics of the stories. Especially when it comes to the opening stories of Creation, the Fall in the garden, the Flood, and the Tower of Babel, we could get caught up in all sorts of ancillary questions. Ultimately, Genesis is not a story of the world in the beginning. It is a story of the God who did the beginning.

Genesis shows us the beauty of creation. And if you look carefully, it reveals the sound of Creation being made. We can hear God breathing in Genesis. In between each of the seven movements of the Creation suite—which the Bible calls "days" but which are not twenty-four--hour periods, but more like movements in a masterpiece—God's voice can be heard above the music and the melody, speaking into the recording each time, "It is good."

So what we see at the end of it all is not just the beauty of creation, but the character of the creator, the heart and soul of the artist. Always be ready to refer back to this opening overture, because everything we will read in the ensuing pages will be founded on what happened in these opening stories, and the redemption that God constantly strives through the pages of Scripture to bring about. This redemption will ultimately come to us in Jesus, but it is a redemption that would enable each of us to work with God to cocreate a future that restores creation to its original purpose.

Genesis 3, with its tale of disobedience and the promise of redemption, offers the great overriding theme that will carry us throughout the Scriptures. That's what we see also in the stories of the Flood and the Tower of Babel. Neither story is very fun. Yet through them, the Holy Spirit washes in as an outward and visible reminder of how God's grace is at work in the human world from the very beginning, to create among us and together with us a future of beauty, goodness, and love. As you read these opening chapters, and as you read the whole Bible, I invite you to prayerfully think about all that Genesis teaches us about God's goodness, about the beauty of creation, and about the special role that you and I get to have in it.

You are part of a creation that has been fashioned by God, and when God made you, God said, "That's good."

DAY 1

Genesis 1:1–3:24

It may come as a surprise, but the Bible says the serpent actually spoke the truth. Some of our hardest temptations aren't lies, but truths. Yes, we can take quick fixes to improve ourselves. But that's at the expense of longing, mystery, and uncertainty. It's part of the beauty of being human.

DAY 2

Genesis 4:1–5:32

The long lists of descendants might seem dry and boring, but notice that the name Enoch is listed twice. Which Enoch will I be today? The descendant of Cain (Genesis 4:17) or the descendant of Seth (Genesis 5:22)? The one whose past and future are characterized by sin and its consequences, or the one who carries forward the story of God's people?

DAY 3 *Genesis 6:1–9:17*

God reboots creation. There are many parallels here with Genesis 1–2, especially between 2:17 and 9:4, where humans have to again avoid the one forbidden thing. Except this time, God introduces something new to humans to help us out: God makes a covenant with all humankind (9:9).

DAY 4 *Genesis 9:18–11:32*

Like Adam and Eve, Noah's nakedness is a metaphor for shame. Like Cain, Ham is the sad recipient of his parents' shame and becomes the ancestor of some of the Bible's worst antagonists. How can I keep shame from being passed on to future generations?

Genesis 12:1–30:43

Pause for a moment and answer this question: Do you have a perfect family?

I'm guessing you answered no. And now that we have that out of the way, let's thank God for the Book of Genesis. Because none of those folks would have raised their hands, either.

An interesting thing happens about a fourth of the way through Genesis. It shifts from the cosmic to the personal. Last week, we read big stories about the grand beginnings of life and the universe. But once we get to chapter 12, the storytelling shifts, away from the cosmic stories of Creation, and the Fall, and the Flood, to the most personal kinds of stories there are: stories about human relationships.

To put it bluntly, the first quarter of Genesis reads like a National Geographic special. But then it shifts to something like a Lifetime Movie of the Week. Or in some cases, the latest drama-filled reality TV show.

Because here is what we learn in Genesis for most of its fifty chapters: human relationships are messy. People are imperfect, and wrestling with each other is part of the human condition.

There is not a single person in Genesis who comes off even remotely smelling like a rose. Every person, including the three that we call the Patriarchs, has weaknesses and shadow sides when it comes to relationships with family and friends.

Abraham—good ol' father Abraham, the ancestor of us all—lies about his wife, Sarah, to save his own skin. Isaac, the child of promise, comes across as passive and indifferent when it comes to his family, as we see in the story of the wells. Jacob is the biggest hoodlum of them all, a trickster and a thief, who cheated his way into inheriting the family bloodline. And Joseph and his brothers? They put the fun in dysfunction. As much as I may have squabbled with my brothers when we were all younger, we never once considered throwing one of us in a pit and selling him off to another household.

In Genesis, there is no perfect person or perfect family. Favoritism, bad parenting, sibling rivalries, and fights over money, inheritance, and fame, all rolled into one gloriously unhealthy family. Imperfection pervades our story from the very beginning.

And yet, as we move through Genesis from beginning to end, we find that in these stories of our ancestors, forgiveness enters the picture. Esau forgives Jacob, and in the next generation, Joseph forgives his brothers.

Yes, relationships with others can be challenging, and it's been that way since the roots of our family tree. But by God's grace, forgiveness is spliced into those roots, and it would be a critical and enduring element that would forever weave its way into the stories of the Bible.

DAY 5

Genesis 12:1–14:24

We are stronger together. Both major crises in today's reading occur when Abram dissolves unity. He subverts his marriage and brings shame to Egypt, then splits from Lot and endangers Lot's life. Both stories reinforce this admonition: maintain fidelity with God, and unity with one another.

DAY 6

Genesis 15:1–17:27

Sometimes we talk to God in the dark. Night is a recurring theme in this text. God meets Abram under the stars, talks to him in a nightmare, and confirms the covenant with flame at night. When we are feeling in the dark, God is closer to us than we even realize.

DAY 7

Genesis 18:1–20:18

God chose not to hide from Abraham what was about to happen to Sodom and Gomorrah, in order to motivate him toward faithfulness. What injustice and sadness will you see today that might prompt you toward faithfulness and love?

DAY 8

Genesis 21:1–23:20

For the first time in Scripture, we see human covenants: between Abraham and Abimelech (Philistine) and Abraham and Ephron (Hittite), representatives of two foreign and often hostile nations. How will you work for peace today, making covenants of reconciliation between hostile parties?

DAY 9

Genesis 24:1–25:18

In today's reading, we meet Isaac's matchmaker. Abraham's servant had a mission to find a mate for Isaac. He was obedient (24:9), prayerful (24:12), and vigilant (24:21). If I am to be that servant today, whom will I meet that can be drawn into an experience of God's love?

DAY 10

Genesis 25:19–28:9

Isaac repeats the deceit of his father Abraham in lying to Abimelech about his wife. Jacob learns from his mother how to deceive his father. These children not only inherit birthrights, but bad traits. What will my offspring, and future generations, learn from me?

DAY 11

Genesis 28:10–30:43

Jacob is tricked by his uncle, marries two of his cousins, has twelve sons by them and two servants. His wives hate each other, and he steals from his uncle: that's how we get the twelve tribes of Israel. Yet despite this family's many flaws, God chooses to work among them.

NOTES & REFLECTIONS

Genesis 31:1–Exodus 12:30

I can remember as a child hearing the story of George Washington chopping down the cherry tree and saying "I cannot tell a lie." I can remember hearing the story of Paul Bunyan, and Babe the Blue Ox, felling trees in the wild frontier. Those were imaginative stories for me as a child, as perhaps they were for you. But now, we can look back and see that they were more than just stories. They helped form the consciousness of our country, teaching us about who we believed we were and what we were called to do.

That is the perfect way to describe the biblical story that we come to now. The story of the Exodus is the single most important story in the entire history of the Israelite people, and one of the most important ones for Christians, second only to Jesus.

It is so significant that for the rest of our journey through the Bible this year, we will lose count of the number of times that the authors of the Bible refer to it. That's how much power the story of the Exodus had in forever shaping the consciousness of an entire culture.

The Exodus would forever remind the Israelites of who they believed God to be, and who they believed they needed to be.

When we end the readings of Genesis, we find that the family of Joseph and his father, Jacob, had moved to Egypt to escape the famine in their homeland. After a long period of time, Jacob's family grew into a massive number of Israelites now living in Egypt. There were so many of them that Pharaoh leveraged them into forced labor to build giant monuments to the gods of Egypt, and they grew so large in number that Pharaoh even tried to control their population by killing off the firstborn of their households.

And it is in that context of forced labor, loss of freedom, excessive punishment, and inhumane treatment that God acted with a mighty hand and an outstretched arm to deliver the people of Israel.

By the time the first act of the Book of Exodus is over, we come to realize why this story is so important to the Israelites, and why it is so important to our faith, and even to the culture of our day. Exodus teaches us that God loves the underdog. God favors the oppressed. We're just three weeks into our journey through the Bible and we have seen this theme many times already. Just like Rebekah favored her younger son Jacob, and Jacob favored his youngest sons Joseph and Benjamin, and even just as God favored the younger brother Abel, God favors the one who is considered inferior. The one who is the victim of injustice, the one who is enslaved.

And that has huge implications for our world and our time today.

As you read this week, ask yourself, in what way is God calling you to work alongside a God who favors the oppressed and seeks justice and equality for all people in our time?

Exodus is not just a story. It is a calling to our conscience. It is a summons to step forward. It is a reminder of what hope looks like.

DAY 12   *Genesis 31:1–36:43*

In today's text, Jacob wrestles with God (Genesis 32:22-32). Jacob's whole life is characterized by both struggle and blessing, in his relationships with others and in his relationship with God. How do struggle and blessing go hand-in-hand in your life?

DAY 13   *Genesis 37:1–41:57*

Young Joseph was bratty and boastful, and his hardships could have made him hardened and bitter. But God did something in him in the pit and in prison. We might only see the immediate struggle, but God can see new life in us over the long haul. How can you claim that hope today?

DAY 14 *Genesis 42:1–45:28*

Somehow Joseph found it in himself to forgive his brothers, and in so doing helped them reconcile with each other ("Do not quarrel along the way," Genesis 45:24 NRSV). A single act of forgiveness can spark healing for wider circles of people. What person is God calling you to forgive today? And from whom should you ask forgiveness?

DAY 15 *Genesis 46:1–50:26*

Jacob and his family are "aliens" who are given asylum in a foreign land. Despite the Egyptians' antipathy to foreigners, they welcome them into their borders. Jacob then "adopts" Joseph's Egyptian sons as his own. These are stories of true hospitality and love and reminders of how we must extend the same to those who feel excluded.

DAY 16 *Exodus 1:1–4:31*

Moses, like Joseph before him, searched for who he was. He was a slave raised in royalty, then was an Egyptian in Midian, then was a fugitive called to be a Hebrew liberator. He was lost until he met I AM. The first one liberated in Exodus was Moses himself. If you're struggling to discover who you really are, how might you find yourself in God?

DAY 17 *Exodus 5:1–7:13*

The idea that the poor are lazy has been used since the days of Pharaoh (5:17). The poor are not lazy. Instead, it is injustice that keeps people down, not their character. That injustice broke the Israelites' spirit (6:9 NRSV) and made them unable to hope.

DAY 18   *Exodus 7:14–12:30*

God knew Pharaoh wouldn't change. So the plagues were not about convincing him, but about emboldening Moses and the broken-spirited Hebrews. It's not about God overcoming pharaohs today, but about God encouraging us to stand up to them. What encouraging word is God giving you today, to fight injustice?

NOTES & REFLECTIONS

Exodus 12:31–34:35

Though it varies depending on the route one takes, the distance between the northern end of the Red Sea and the Jordan River is around 250 miles. For the Israelites in the Book of Exodus, that was the straight shot, the shortest distance between Egypt, the land of slavery, and Canaan, the land God promised to their ancestors.

If you figure that the average person can walk about twenty-five miles a day with enough time to rest at night, that means the Israelites could have made that journey from slavery to the Promised Land in ten days. Even at a third of that speed, it would have taken around one month. But instead, that journey took forty years through the wilderness. Forty long years of wandering and wondering through the desert.

There are a couple of practical reasons why. For one thing, a straight shot from Egypt to Canaan would have brought them right through the territory of enemies, and likely to battle against those enemies (13:17-18). Second, God led the people to Mount Sinai to meet with them and make a covenant with them (chapters 19–24). But regardless of the route, a journey from Egypt to Canaan should by no means take forty years. There must be some other explanation for the time the Israelites spent in the wilderness.

The reason is a theological one: the road to forming character as God's people, the road to developing faithfulness to God, and the process of becoming a loving, trusted community takes time. There are no shortcuts to spiritual formation.

If the journey between Egypt and Canaan were filled with roads and cities, street signs and maps, then the Israelites could have very easily relied on their abilities to get to where they wanted to go. Instead, the very first thing they had to come to grips with—at the very moment the Red Sea fell back on itself and swallowed Pharaoh's army—was the fact that they had no clue where to go next. Remember that none of them besides Moses had ever been outside Egypt before. They had no idea what to do next.

They had no choice but to follow the giant cloud that God used to lead them during the day, and the pillar of fire that led them at night. They did not have the luxury of knowing where they would be tomorrow or next week or next month. All they had was the present moment, the task at hand, the gift of today.

In Exodus, we read how God gave the Israelites enough in every present moment to make it, one day at a time. God gave the Israelites just enough food to eat in the form of manna, bread that came down from heaven. God gave them quails that they could catch. God gave them the laws and a covenant to guide their life together. And God even gave them a tangible, physical reminder of God's constant presence with them, in the form of a Tabernacle: a portable, elaborate tent, only 700 square feet, not much bigger than a one-bedroom apartment. But inside that small tent, they knew that God was with them.

God had given them just enough, every day, in every way.

DAY 19　　　　*Exodus 12:31–15:21*

Life isn't filled with daily Red Sea miracles. But it does have clouds by day and pillars of fire by night. These are steady, reliable reminders of God's presence. Anxious Israelites only had to watch for those when they needed encouragement. We can, too, if we will take notice of the glimpses of God's presence that are all around us.

DAY 20　　　　*Exodus 15:22–18:27*

Mount Horeb (also known as Mount Sinai) is a special place: it's the location of God's burning bush for Moses, God's still, small voice to Elijah, and here, God's fresh water for complaining Israelites. Horeb symbolizes God's presence, available throughout our lives, even when we feel like we are in the desert. What will your Mount Horeb be today?

DAY 21   *Exodus 19:1–21:36*

So many of the laws in Exodus 21 seem antiquated and irrelevant today. But they do remind us that being God's people means treating others with respect and fairness and that God cares about every aspect of our lives and our relationships with those around us.

DAY 22   *Exodus 22:1–24:18*

God promises brighter days ahead, but in increments, not fell swoops (Exodus 23:29-30). God clears the obstacles for joy gradually, rather than all at once, so that we can develop the disciplines to live into that joy. What evidence do you see of God's steady and subtle work of grace in your life?

DAY 23 *Exodus 25:1–27:21*

As elaborate and impressive as the Tabernacle was, it came entirely from material the Israelites had on hand (25:1-7) We often tend to focus on our shortcomings, but God has already given us everything we need to live.

DAY 24 *Exodus 28:1–30:38*

Here are more than a hundred verses of explicit instructions on what the priests were to wear and do. It may feel like lots of trivial tedium. But it reminds us that God is pleased by the rhythm and consistency of our spiritual disciplines. Here are seven spiritual disciplines that accompany and enrich the Christian life: worship, small groups, service, giving financially, reading Scripture, inviting others, and prayer. Which ones do you need to improve on?

DAY 25 *Exodus 31:1–34:35*

The fact that the Lord changed his mind might offer an unsettling view of God, but it is a liberating view of prayer. Moses and God could talk to each other as friends (33:11). That means God listens, and our prayers make a difference to God. How might that truth change the way you pray?

NOTES & REFLECTIONS

Exodus 35:1–Leviticus 23:44

The final six chapters of Exodus relate the building of the Tabernacle and instruments of worship: the tent and its courtyard, the ark of the covenant, the table and lampstand, incense altar, the altar for burnt offerings, and the clothing for the priests. The description of their construction closely echoes God's instructions for building them in Exodus 25–30. On the one hand, this can seem needlessly repetitive to us as we read it. On the other hand, however, it highlights the exactness and attention with which the Israelites followed God's instructions. They built it just as God said, assuring that their worship of God would be faithful and authentic and that they would fully recognize God's holy presence among them. This idea is reinforced by the repeated statement that they did things "as the Lord had commanded Moses," and it is confirmed by God's presence filling the Tabernacle as Exodus closes. Such detailed instruction shows the great care that accompanies God's holiness, which stands at the center of Israel's worship and their very identity as God's people.

The same level of precision and detail continues into Leviticus, which begins with directions for offering sacrifices, followed by the consecration of Aaron and his sons as priests and the beginning of worship. After that are directions of ritual purification and the annual Day of Reconciliation (also known as the Day of Atonement) in chapter 16. The first sixteen chapters of Leviticus contain instructions that pertain mostly to the priests, such as the proper way to offer sacrifices. Beginning with chapter 17, however, the book's scope turns to all of the Israelites, guiding them in their conduct. Often called the "Holiness Code" in biblical scholarship, Leviticus 17–27 suggests that observing holiness is not just the purview of priests, but a responsibility for all the Israelite people. God called the Israelites to be "a kingdom of priests" and "a holy nation" (Exodus 19:6). The laws we find in Exodus, Leviticus, and Deuteronomy guide them in living as God's holy people.

Many find these chapters challenging to read; it's as if we are reading an ancient instruction manual, which, in many ways, we are. We won't understand all of the details, and we likely will struggle to see how these directions apply to our lives today that are different in so many ways from the ancient Israelite community. But they are a reminder for us that God cares about the details of our lives and that discipleship involves careful, consistent obedience. As you read, bear in mind the witness of the ancient Israelites and their priests who both observed God's instructions and preserved them for us today. How does their faithfulness inspire you to do the little things well in your walk with God?

DAY 26

Exodus 35:1–40:38

Exodus closes with God smacking Pharaoh one last time. No matter how beautiful the buildings were that the Israelites built for Pharaoh, they were nothing compared to the grandeur and beautiful detail of the Tabernacle. When God's people work together, amazing things can happen. What will you build for God today with the help of others?

DAY 27

Leviticus 1:1–4:35

The sacrificial system seems so antiquated, especially with its gory, bloody details. But it's a reminder that God requires our very best, even when things are going well. Discipleship is found in doing the little things well, consistently.

DAY 28
Leviticus 5:1–7:38

Leviticus is about mulligans. Do-overs. The sacrificial system in ancient Israel acknowledges that we will mess up, and gives us a chance to start over. Though we no longer offer animal sacrifices today, the main idea is still true: God offers us chances to get it right, and make it right. What do you need to repent from today, and how might you experience God's forgiveness today?

DAY 29
Leviticus 8:1–10:20

Aaron goes from the high of God's calling to the low of God's holy wrath and the death of his sons. His silent reaction (10:3) is haunting. Following God involves high reward and high cost, joy and grief. In that silence, we wrestle with God.

DAY 30 *Leviticus 11:1–14:57*

The purity laws remind us that sin is pervasive, that it requires vigilance to detect and avoid, and that God's grace can cleanse us through repentance, ritual, and the love of community. Those truths are still the same today.

DAY 31 *Leviticus 15:1–18:30*

Still haunted by the sins of his sons and the pain of their death, Aaron releases the scapegoat into the wilderness with the people's sins, the goat symbolically bearing away their iniquities. May you experience God's forgiveness in this same way: your sins cast far and out of sight, and may you forgive others in the same way.

DAY 32

Leviticus 19:1–23:44

You don't need to be perfect for God to love you. You need to love God because God is perfect. And that means offering to God your very best.

NOTES & REFLECTIONS

Leviticus 24:1–Numbers 21:35

After wandering through the wilderness, the Israelites were so close—so very close—to entering the Promised Land. It had been a long, hot, treacherous journey. But they had made it this far, thanks in large part to their tenacity, but mostly due to God's generosity. God had given them food and drink to sustain them, just enough to go one day at a time. God had given them rules to love and live by, in the form of the commandments, which we heard about in Leviticus last week. God had given them the Tabernacle, the visible, unmistakable reminder of God's presence with them.

But most of all, God had given them clear direction as to where to go. A formidable cloud moved ahead of them by day, and a tall pillar of fire moved ahead of them by night. All they had to do was follow it, keep up with it, never move ahead of it, and they would be confident in their progress toward their destination.

Then at the start of Numbers 13, that all changed.

They were now just miles away from the border of the Promised Land, and what is implied in this text is that there would no longer be a daily cloud or nightly fire to lead them.

God decided instead to take the training wheels off, to see if they could decide what to do next on their own.

God told Moses to select twelve men to scout out the Promised Land and bring back a report. Why, do you suppose God had them do that? Obviously, God knew what they would find. They would find sprawling armies filled with giant soldiers next to whom the Israelites would appear like tiny grasshoppers. Yes, they would find a bounty of produce, a land rich with milk and honey, a veritable paradise awaiting them. But they would also see the kinds of ominous threats that would trigger a cautious person.

The obvious answer would appear to be that this was a test. A test by God to see if they would trust in God, rather than the evidence. A test to see if they would live by faith, and not by the data.

But digging a little deeper, we might see that this was not just about the decision itself, but how they would make that decision. Ten of the twelve spies came back reporting the truth. The threats are ominous, the chances of survival are slim.

Only Joshua and Caleb, representing the minority report, looked at the data and offered truth as well. God was with them, and that's all that mattered.

These were competing truths, and the people had to decide.

Here's the lesson that is crystal clear in this story: Humility is always right. Generosity of spirit is always right. Courage is always right, when it is unpaired from arrogance. Truth is something to be pursued and never something to be owned.

And I suppose the final lesson is this: God's got this. God always sees the long game, even when we can't.

DAY 33 *Leviticus 24:1–27:34*

If only sabbath, sabbatical years, and jubilee were more observed in today's world. It would renew our energies, restore our land and economies, and repair our relationships. How might you incorporate sabbath practices in your days, weeks, months, and years?

DAY 34 *Numbers 1:1–4:49*

Teamwork makes God's dream work. Each Levite had a vital role to play to ensure the worship of God. Thank God for the ministry of the people in your life and congregation. What is the key role in the church that God is calling you to play?

DAY 35   *Numbers 5:1–7:89*

This is the benediction that many have learned: "The LORD bless you and keep you. The LORD make his face shine on you and be gracious to you. The LORD lift up his face to you and grant you peace" (6:24-26). What do these verses mean to you?

DAY 36   *Numbers 8:1–10:36*

Numbers 9 reminds us of what God has done in our shared past (Passover) and what God can do in our shared future (cloud and fire). The spiritual life is a dynamic tension between remembering and following. Think about the key moments in your life when God did great things. What does that suggest about how God might work in your future?

DAY 37 *Numbers 11:1–14:45*

Nearly every hard emotion is in this reading: discontentment, sadness, jealousy, fear, and anger. Some of those emotions even come from God! It reminds us that every close relationship has bad days. Even the life of faith has dark nights of the soul.

DAY 38 *Numbers 15:1–18:32*

The offerings were mainly for praising God and confessing to God. But the people wanted personal access, the ability to make requests directly of God. The fact that we can do that today should humble us, not make us feel entitled.

DAY 39 *Numbers 19:1–21:35*

It's easy to sympathize with the thirsty, desperate Israelites in their quarrel with God at Meribah. God provided, only after reminding them they weren't God. Quarrels with God are natural and permissible; we just need to remember we aren't God.

NOTES & REFLECTIONS

Numbers 22:1–Deuteronomy 16:22

If you had the opportunity, right now, to go back in time twenty years ago, and have a conversation with that version of yourself twenty years younger, what would you say to that person? What would you tell your ten-year-old self? Your teenage self? Or your young adult self?

Deuteronomy was not written at the time of the Exodus. It was written some eight hundred years later, by a future generation of God's people, as a message to their younger selves.

That older version of the Israelites will have gone through a lot in those eight hundred years after they entered the Promised Land. They will have conquered the Canaanites and settled into the Promised Land (which we will read about in the Book of Joshua). They will go through ups and downs in their faithfulness to God (which we will read about in Judges).

And then they will ask for a king, because all of the other empires have one. So, they will get Saul and David and Solomon, the first three kings of the monarchy, which we will read about in 1–2 Samuel and 1 Kings and 1 Chronicles.

And then the kingdom will fall apart. They will become so polarized as a country that they will fracture into two. The Northern Kingdom will meet their fate when they are scattered by the Assyrian Empire. And in 586 BCE, some eight centuries after the Israelites first entered the Promised Land, the Southern Kingdom will crumble. The Babylonian Empire will rise, take them captive, and whisk them away into exile.

The name *Deuteronomy* literally means, "Second Law." It is a reiteration, a reminder, of everything the older Israelites would want to remember about what is most important.

Deuteronomy takes the form of Moses preaching his very last sermons to the Israelites in the wilderness before he died. A reminder of all the rituals, customs, and festivals that God had given them, but also a reminder of what was important.

Moses tells them, You are going to go through hard times, Israel. But stay faithful. Live with integrity. Walk in the one-way direction, the way God wants you to walk.

> *What does the LORD your God ask of you? Only this: to revere the*
> *LORD your God by walking in all his ways, by loving him, by serving the*
> *LORD your God with all your heart and being, and by keeping the LORD's*
> *commandments . . . So, circumcise your hearts and stop being so stubborn.*
> (*Deuteronomy 10:12-13, 16*)

These are not just words from the past, in an ancient, dusty book from long ago. The structure of Deuteronomy suggests that these are words from our future selves, reminding you that while there is sure to be heartache and suffering that is yet to unfold in your future, there is one thing you can control: You can stay true. You can remain steadfast in your love and trust of God. You can choose to remain faithful to doing the right thing even when it is costly. You can live a life of integrity even when it is easier to compromise your principles. And you can stay in the one-way direction of God's path, even when the other way is wider and more popular.

DAY 40 *Numbers 22:1–25:18*

The story of Balaam and Balak reminds us that prayer is neither selective hearing or selective speaking. We must be open to receiving from God what we don't want to hear. And, we must be faithful to say what we are reluctant to say.

DAY 41 *Numbers 26:1–31:54*

Moses not being allowed to enter the Promised Land can seem like a cruel irony. But he was at least given a remarkable consolation prize. It was the view of the land from afar, the ability to see a future he could not claim, but he helped carve. Our actions today help make an impact we may not see. But it is a privilege to work toward that future.

DAY 42 *Numbers 32:1–36:13*

God ordered nothing less than the complete conquest of Canaan. Likewise, God wants nothing less than the complete spiritual makeover of our lives and the world. Any remaining injustices or sins will be "thorns in your side" (33:55). How willing are you to surrender your life completely over to God?

DAY 43 *Deuteronomy 1:1–4:49*

Deuteronomy may have been written in part during the Exile. So, when your life and the world around you seem in exile, far removed from what it can and should be, Deuteronomy reminds you of this: stay faithful (4:3).

DAY 44   *Deuteronomy 5:1–8:20*

Jesus, like the Israelites, was tested in the wilderness. This reading from Deuteronomy contains all three of his responses to the devil (5:9; 6:16; 8:3). Jesus drew strength from God's faithfulness, just as God had instructed the Israelites. God can do the same for you if you will allow God to.

DAY 45   *Deuteronomy 9:1–12:32*

God knew that the spoils of victory could make the Israelites forgetful and boastful. Change for the better can be as challenging to the spiritual life as change for the worse. Your faith is tested in the good times and in the bad.

DAY 46 *Deuteronomy 13:1–16:22*

The law required putting to death those who would sway us from God. That sounds super harsh. But it is language that Paul uses in Colossians 3:5: "Put to death the parts of your life that belong to the earth." God takes seriously that which lures us away.

NOTES & REFLECTIONS

Deuteronomy 17:1–Joshua 11:23

The Book of Joshua is a story that we have to handle with great care. On the one hand, it can transform your life for the better. On the other hand, it also has the potential for causing great harm. It is the biblical equivalent of nitroglycerin. Handled with care, it can heal. Handled carelessly, it is explosive and dangerous.

Let's start with the encouragement first. You don't have to go too far into the book before you realize that one of its central themes is *courage*. God says, "Be brave and strong." Do not be fearful or dismayed, God says, for I am with you.

It's exactly what the Israelites needed to hear. After being slaves in Egypt for four hundred years, after wandering in the wilderness for forty years, after the great liberator Moses had died, these Israelites probably felt like they were the worst equipped to take on the challenge of claiming the Promised Land. They were wanderers, not warriors. They were the conquered, not the conquerors.

Remember: throughout the Bible, God made a habit of defying the odds. In God's hands, the Red Sea became a sidewalk. The walls of Jericho became Jenga blocks. Later, a giant would be slain by a slingshot. By the time we get to the Gospels, a boulder would become as a bowling ball, and a tomb would become a triumph. In the face of fear, God is greater than the odds.

But this story alone beckons more from us than just courage. If we take a serious look at the Book of Joshua, we have to confront some of the troubling aspects of its stories, and we have to figure out how to take the Bible seriously, without taking it literally.

Joshua and Judges are the bloodiest books in the entire Bible. But it is not just the violence that is the most troubling to our modern ears. It is the idea—the dangerous idea—that victory is always proof that God is on our side.

How would the story of Joshua read to an indigenous people who have been decimated and evicted from their tribal lands?

How would the story of Joshua read to victims of domestic violence, in which the abusers believe that because they have the power, they have the right?

How would the story of Joshua read to people who are suffering from the effects of global climate change, because of the human notion that this world is ours to conquer for our own advancement?

These are very hard questions. We have to be very careful with Scriptures like these, which is why I believe reading the Bible, gaining familiarity with it, is so important. Because only by reading through these texts in order can we learn how to separate the beauty from the harm, which can only come from taking the Bible seriously, but not always literally.

So, what do we do with Joshua? Well, I would suggest that while courage is a central theme in the book, courage must be tempered with good judgment, and especially by faithfulness and humility. If there is anything that the Bible teaches us over and over again, it's that pride is the surest pathway to self-destruction. God calls us in Joshua to face our future without fear, not so that we may conquer, but so that we may obey and follow God without reservation.

DAY 47   *Deuteronomy 17:1–20:20*

For the first time we hear about kings and prophets, further evidence that Deuteronomy was written during the monarchy and the Exile. Neither office supersedes God. We must never trust earthly rulers to give us what only God can provide: eternal security, ultimate purpose, everlasting contentment, and joy.

DAY 48   *Deuteronomy 21:1–25:19*

Today's reading is filled with laws that seem entirely archaic and antiquated. It's impossible to imagine taking them all literally today, which is a reminder that faithful Bible reading should allow for reason and experience, not just tradition.

DAY 49   *Deuteronomy 26:1–30:20*

If unchecked, Deuteronomy 28 can lead to vending machine theology (God blesses me when I do good) or bad theodicy (suffering happens because of me). Instead, we should be motivated by covenant (chap. 29). We love, because God first loved us.

DAY 50   *Deuteronomy 31:1–34:12*

Moses gives a final reminder to heed God's commandments and a reminder that God is with them and goes before them no matter what. And then he dies in peace. Would it be that we all finish our journeys just as strong as Moses did.

DAY 51   *Joshua 1:1–3:17*

The crossing of the Jordan is referenced in our baptismal liturgy, as a reminder of how God is present and powerful through the symbol of water. Joshua 1:9 reminds us to "be brave and strong," not alarmed or dismayed, because God is with us. What difference does your baptism make in the way you face your challenges?

DAY 52   *Joshua 4:1–6:27*

Before the Israelites conquered Jericho, they remembered who they were (circumcision), remembered what God had done (Passover), and remembered their new responsibilities (cultivate and eat the produce of the land). How might you remember your identity in God, your blessings from God, and your responsibilities to God?

DAY 53

Joshua 7:1–11:23

The story of Achan reminds us that the truth always comes to light. Hidden sins don't stay hidden forever, and they affect many innocent victims. Help us, Lord, be true to you, even when we think no one is watching.

NOTES & REFLECTIONS

Joshua 12:1–Judges 16:31

If I were to summarize the Book of Judges in one word, it would be the word *cycle*. And if I were to summarize the difficulty of leading the Christian life, I would use the very same word.

In the film *Groundhog Day*, Bill Murray plays a news weather personality assigned to cover the annual Groundhog Day festivities in Punxsutawney, Pennsylvania. He discovers over the course of several days that he is actually reliving the same day, over and over again.

At first, this is a great thing for him. He can make a mistake, even do things wrong on purpose, take huge risks, and have a clean slate the next morning. But then, after a while, he discovers that living in a cycle that you cannot stop is a source of true suffering.

He cannot break loose. He is condemned to live each day just as before. He repeats the same mistakes, suffers the same agonies, is haunted by the same guilt, and is followed by the same hurts.

In a way, *Groundhog Day* is an accurate metaphor for the cyclical nature of the human condition. We, too, are trapped in a seemingly inescapable, sinful routine. For a while, we are faithful and obedient. And then temptation comes. We break away from God's best, and find ourselves in a hardship of our own creation. Then we cry out to God for help, and find our way back to obedience, only to slip back to our old ways again. And again. And again.

And that cyclical pattern of sin is exactly what the Book of Judges is all about.

The Israelites have now conquered the Promised Land and have settled into their twelve tribal communities. They are now free and self-sufficient, no longer wanderers, no longer slaves.

But they have forgotten the one important thing: to live as God has commanded. To live a holy and pure life, obedient to the ways of God. Instead, they live a vicious cycle of obedience and disobedience.

At first, they are doing well: doing the right thing, staying true to God. And then they lapse. They fall into disobedience, failing to love God and put God first, choosing to bring harm to one another. So God sends them a course correction, usually in the form of an army from the outside who sweeps in and conquers them. The Israelites then hit rock bottom, and they cry to God for help, in repentance for what they have done wrong.

So God sends a deliverer. The Hebrew Bible called them "judges," not because they were administrators of the legal system, but because they were strong, charismatic, temporary leaders who conquered the opposing forces.

There are Deborah and Jael, the leaders who remind us of the power of women.

There is Gideon, who reminds us that God can use anyone, no matter how insignificant they seem.

There is Samson, who reminds us that it was his integrity, not his hair, that was the ultimate source of his strength.

Twelve judges total, twelve moments of deliverance by God. And then, for a period of time, there was peace again. Until the next time they sinned.

The Book of Judges reminds us that sin is something we need to combat every day, not just one time. It requires daily diligence, a daily choice to get right with God.

DAY 54

Joshua 12:1–17:18

The Israelites underwent a significant identity change. From nomadic warriors to settlers. From a life on the move to life on the land. It's a crucial life transition too: learning to bloom where you are planted, not being itchy to move on. How might God be calling you and equipping you to live with contentment today?

DAY 55

Joshua 18:1–24:33

The long lists of borders and geography seem tedious, but it underscores two points: God was faithful to deliver what God promised to the Israelites, and God made room for everyone to be part of God's household. There is hope in both ideas. How do God's faithfulness and God's love for all make a difference in the way you see the world and its problems?

DAY 56 *Judges 1:1–3:6*

Sin is a result of forgetfulness (as Christian theologian Richard Rohr explains): a forgetfulness of who God is or of what we are called to be. God provided the Israelites with judges to serve as reminders. What will God send us today to remind us how to be faithful? We need to be attentive to those whom God has summoned today to deliver us and call us to faithfulness. Who are those people for you?

DAY 57 *Judges 3:7–5:31*

The story of Deborah is a timely reminder that God's voice of power and liberation can come from any person, regardless of their background or our expectations of them. All we have to do is listen to them, stay with them, and go with them (4:8). Who in your mind is a Deborah for our time?

DAY 58 *Judges 6:1–8:35*

The story of Gideon reminds us that God doesn't need quantity, numbers advantages, or power games to make things happen. God just needs obedient hearts willing to struggle and stay faithful for the long haul. A timely message, to be sure.

DAY 59 *Judges 9:1–12:15*

The stories of Abimelech and Jephthah remind us of the perils of lusting for power. When you crave it, you'll do anything to get it. And when you have it, you don't realize what it has done to you. The power of love is greater than loveless power.

DAY 60 *Judges 13:1–16:31*

The secret of Samson's strength was his hair. But the test of Samson's strength was his integrity. It doesn't matter how much charisma one has in public if one is compromised in private.

NOTES & REFLECTIONS

Judges 17:1–1 Samuel 15:35

The story of Ruth comes at just the right time to restore our faith in humanity. The story of Ruth comes along like a warm blanket or an oasis in the desert.

If the Bible were to stop at the Book of Judges, you would think that the Israelites would never figure it out. If it were to stop now, we would come to the conclusion that committing acts of violence is the chief way to demonstrate your obedience to God. That seems to be the overriding theme of Joshua and Judges.

Then along comes Ruth. It's the most surprising story, and it comes at just the perfect time. As the story unfolds, we meet a woman named Naomi. She is blessed with a husband and two boys, enough to guarantee a comfortable and secure life in her world. But then, in an instant, her world changed. In the first five verses, both her husband and her two sons died.

The only thing worse than grief is a grief that is mixed with fear. Not only did Naomi lose her closest family members, she lost her social and economic safety net. She lost her means of income and the guarantee of her survival. If the story had ended here, this very likely would have been the end of Naomi, just as it is for countless people in our world for whom one unsuspecting tragedy sends them down a spiral that they cannot get out of.

But notice something remarkable: even in her misery, Naomi still puts the needs of others first. She realized that there are two other people in her life who are grieving. They are the wives of her two sons, and these women also are now widows. Her daughters-in-law are named Orpah and Ruth.

And we can imagine Naomi choking back her own tears, presenting a facade of toughness and strength, as she said to those two young women, I'll be fine. Really, I'll be okay. You have your whole life ahead of you. Go back to the homes where you came from. Get married again, start over, and don't worry about me. Really.

What a decision for Orpah and Ruth. Orpah decides to leave. And we can't blame her. Honestly, she's hurting, and she probably considers this less about turning her back on Naomi and more about turning toward healing and hope. We get it.

But Ruth chooses a different path. The hard path. The path of loyalty. Despite Naomi's urging, Ruth insists on staying with her. And it's here, in the story of Ruth, that we get the most basic definition of biblical loyalty: I'm not leaving you. I'll be right here. I'm with you.

The story of Ruth could not come at a better time. Judges ends with some of the most difficult and graphically violent stories in the Bible. And the Book of 1 Samuel reads like a continuation of Judges, as the people of Israel make a transition from temporary, charismatic military leadership to a permanent monarchy.

Then, just as we might come to the conclusion that being obedient involves violence and power, and being in community involves betrayal and harm, along comes a story that reminds us of what it means to live with godly character.

The story of Ruth reminds us of the qualities of faithfulness that we may have forgotten were a part of the biblical narrative.

Ruth is a reminder of the Bible's best qualities: of care for the oppressed, concern for the outsider, and love for all people, especially those who are down and out. These qualities will remain vital for those who rule Israel, as we find in the first chapters of 1 Samuel.

DAY 61 *Judges 17:1–21:25*

Civil war breaks out among the tribes over the inhumane treatment of a person deemed second-class in society. Thousands of lives lost, and heartbreaking division. But it ends with reconciliation and compassion, albeit imperfect, and a new future. What meaning do you derive from these stories for today?

DAY 62 *Ruth 1:1–2:23*

Sometimes, when times are darkest and you feel most hopeless, the most beautiful words that someone can tell you are, "Wherever you go, I will go." And it's the best thing you can tell someone else. What can the story of Ruth and Naomi teach you about loyalty and fidelity?

DAY 63 *Ruth 3:1–4:22*

The story of Ruth (a Moabite) ends with her genealogy. She was the grandmother of David, ancestor of Jesus. It's a reminder that even in the family tree of Jesus, there is room for foreigners and immigrants. What do you think that means for us today?

DAY 64 *1 Samuel 1:1–3:21*

Samuel was born into a world of grief. Hannah grieved her barrenness, Eli grieved his wayward sons, and the people were without divine vision. But the call of Samuel brought hope, and his obedience came in the words, "I'm here." How might you claim those words and be open to God?

DAY 65   *1 Samuel 4:1–7:17*

God is not a lucky rabbit's foot, or vending machine, or cosmic butler that can meet our desires on demand. Nor can God be captured and contained by any one tribe. God not only loves all, but reigns over all. To get that wrong is to do harm. What difference does this insight make to you?

DAY 66   *1 Samuel 8:1–12:25*

The anointing of Saul is God saying to the Israelites more or less, I'll give you what you want, but you really don't know what you're asking for. God often cares more about what we need, and less about what we want, because what we want isn't always best.

DAY 67

1 Samuel 13:1–15:35

Saul's impatience and ego distorted true service to God into self-promotion. He was also so busy being a warrior that he left little time to be a spiritual leader (14:35). He lost his kingship because he made it about himself, not God. Is there a part of you that can relate to Saul in this way?

NOTES & REFLECTIONS

1 Samuel 16:1–2 Samuel 7:29

The Book of Judges is one story after another of invading armies that threatened the Israelites' livelihood and well-being. For a while, the Israelites would feel they had it contained, but then the cycle of sin and its consequences reset. More invasion, more oppression, more crying out to God. Those years must have felt for the Israelites what the year 2020 felt like for many of us. In the wake of a global pandemic, with loss and uncertainty and disruption, I think now I understand better than ever before why the Israelites felt like they wanted a king. It wasn't jealousy of the other empires. That's what I always thought it was: All the other nations have one, why can't we?

No. Instead, I think what they really wanted was stability. Comfort. Some semblance of routine. A sense of the familiar. That's what a king represented for them. When the Israelites said, We want a king, what they were really saying was, We want a sense of steadiness in the face of uncertainty. We want this roller coaster to stop.

And they thought they had one, for a while. They thought God had given them exactly what they needed in their first king, King Saul. He was a strong, charismatic force of nature, who conquered all their enemies and gave them victories. They thought it was just what the doctor ordered.

But over time, they would learn something about Saul: looks can be deceiving. And those things that you thought you could turn to for comfort and normalcy don't always last.

So, as God often does in situations like this, God gave the Israelites a second chance to learn an important lesson and to get it right. They needed a reminder of what is most important in times of uncertainty, times like these. A reminder that God always gives just what we need, something special for times like these.

And that critical, key lesson came to them from the most surprising person, the person you would least expect to offer strength and encouragement, based on his outward appearance.

David was a young kid, a singing shepherd, the furthest thing from a king. But the prophet Samuel's words to Jesse, David's father, were clear: "God doesn't look at things like humans do. Humans see only what is visible to the eyes, but the LORD sees into the heart" (1 Samuel 16:7).

What is it that David teaches us? The character of a faithful person. The ability to trust God with our whole heart. To trust God with the part of our selves that no one else can see. To love, serve, and worship God, regardless of our circumstances.

No, David wasn't perfect. Yes, he made some major-league mistakes. But God used him to show the Israelites the very thing that God wants to share with us: your character, your commitment to God, and your love for others are what matter most.

DAY 68   *1 Samuel 16:1–17:58*

David conquered two foes: the one within Saul's darkened spirit and the external enemy of Goliath. He defeated the first with peace and music, and the second with strength. Jesus said we need to be wise as serpents and gentle as doves. David was both. How might you discover and practice balance between the two?

DAY 69   *1 Samuel 18:1–20:42*

As Saul's anger grew stronger for David, so did Jonathan's love for him. It's the story of the human condition: hate vs. love, jealousy vs. goodwill, violence vs. peace. May we be more like Jonathan and less like Saul in our interactions with others.

DAY 70   *1 Samuel 21:1–24:22*

Ahimelech shows mercy on David, and a vengeful Saul makes him pay with his life. David shows mercy on Saul and spares his life. The contrast couldn't be more stark. Revenge perpetuates violence. Forgiveness ends it. What difference should that make to you?

DAY 71   *1 Samuel 25:1–28:25*

Abigail and Achish both show hospitality to David, saving his life from Saul, exhibiting great risk in doing so. How might we create bridges rather than walls with those who are our perceived enemies today?

DAY 72   *1 Samuel 29:1–31:13*

This is a major low point for David: Amalekites stole his soldiers' family members, as well as two of his own family, and the people turned against him. But he strengthened himself in God (30:6) and pressed on to recover what was lost. Let this be a good reminder to trust in God today.

DAY 73   *2 Samuel 1:1–4:12*

The transition from Saul to David was ugly and violent. David was a shepherd who learned to be a warrior, and then he had to learn to govern. He saw that the first step in bringing people together was to teach them how to grieve (3:35-36). What does healthy grieving look like to you, and why is that important?

DAY 74

2 Samuel 5:1–7:29

There are many reasons why we ought to pray for an end to religious violence. David's violence established Jerusalem, but God would later deem him too violent to build the Temple. May God's peace prevail over violence in God's name. How will you be a conduit for that peace?

NOTES & REFLECTIONS

2 Samuel 8:1–1 Kings 11:43

As far as biblical characters go, Solomon is one of the most complicated. He did so many things right at the beginning of his rule as king over Israel, following his father, David. Yet he wound up doing so many things wrong.

At the start of Solomon's reign, God came to Solomon and said, "Ask whatever you wish, and I'll give it to you" (1 Kings 3:5). Oh, and by the way, God said that to him in a dream. I think that's important. Because oftentimes, what we dream about at night is a reflection of what we are worrying about during the day. And I can imagine that as part of that dream, Solomon was really wrestling with all the chaos in his life at that moment.

His father had just died. There was backstabbing political drama all around him. The burden of leading this nation was weighing heavily on him. He worried about it during the day, and he wrestled over it in his dreams.

If God were to come to us in the midst of that sheet-tossing, bed-rolling kind of dream and say, "Hello, my child, what would you like me to give you?" I wonder what you and I would say.

Would you ask for your problems to go away?

Would you ask for your enemies to disappear?

Would you ask for a strong economy, for health and peace of mind, for comfort, for power?

Is that what it means to "trust in God"?

As it turns out, Solomon didn't ask for any of those things. He asked for something deeper and richer and even more meaningful. He asked for wisdom. He asked for "a discerning mind in order to govern your people and to distinguish good from evil" (3:9).

Here's why that's important. Solomon realized that what really defines a life well lived is not the big moments, not the huge ups and downs, not the glories or the crises, but the daily things. The little decisions. The small and subtle moments when we choose how we are going to respond and how we are going to think and feel.

Solomon wasn't asking for knowledge or book smarts or intellect.

He wanted to know how to live well, when things were going great, when things were going badly, and every kind of moment in between. That's what it meant for him to trust in God.

He was asking for an ability to see that fine line between living the good, moral, and upright life, and a life of chaos, harm, and futility. He recognized that regardless of whatever was happening out in the world, whatever is happening with pandemics and stock markets and local economies, when it all comes down to it, we still have the gift of choice.

We have the ability to choose how we will respond, how we will act, how we will think and feel.

We can choose whether we will stay the course of good, peace, calm, and centeredness, or stumble into a path of chaos, greed, panic, and paralyzing fear.

That is the difference between good and evil. For Solomon, that is at the heart of wisdom. That is what it means to trust in God.

DAY 75   *2 Samuel 8:1–10:19*

On the outside, David is successful and victorious. On the inside, he is still heartbroken over the loss of Jonathan. It's like a game of Would You Rather: Would you rather defeat all your enemies or keep all your friends? Perhaps David would choose the latter. How about you?

DAY 76   *2 Samuel 11:1–14:33*

David's sin is not only found out; it casts a long shadow on his family. His children devolve into abuse and aggression, and his house becomes rife with conflict. How will the consequences of our sins impact future generations?

DAY 77 *2 Samuel 15:1–19:43*

The conflict between David and Absalom had to be the low point of David's life. David grieved over his rebellious son's death, just as any parents would mourn the bad choices of their children. David kept his throne, but it cost him greatly. What can we learn from this episode in David's life?

DAY 78 *2 Samuel 20:1–24:25*

The close of David's reign is filled with more uprising, settling of scores, and a sinful display of arrogance. David was not perfect, but he tried to keep his focus and praise on God (chapters 22–23). What can you do to keep your focus on serving and worshipping God?

DAY 79   *1 Kings 1:1–4:34*

In 1 Kings 3:5-9 is Solomon's prayer for "a discerning mind" and the ability to "distinguish good from evil." It is a humble, noble request, one that ought to be more displayed by our spiritual and civic leaders today.

DAY 80   *1 Kings 5:1–8:66*

The longest prayer so far offered by a person to God is in 1 Kings 8:23-53. Solomon appeals to God for mercy, justice, and forgiveness. It is a reminder that the Temple itself was not the object of worship, but the means to worship God. How can Solomon's prayer shape what you pray for?

DAY 81 $\qquad$ *1 Kings 9:1–11:43*

Here we see the rise and fall of Solomon in three chapters. You could have all the riches, pedigrees, influence, and intellect in the world, but without a moral compass that is consistent with God's best, it can all be torn to shreds.

NOTES & REFLECTIONS

1 Kings 12:1–2 Kings 17:41

In this week's set of Scriptures, we read about the two prophets in the Northern Kingdom, Elijah and Elisha. The stories of Elijah and Elisha are inspiring, comforting, and encouraging. Long before the book *Chicken Soup for the Soul* was written, there were these stories from 1 Kings. If we pay close attention to these stories, especially 1 Kings 17–19, we discover that God gives us enough, that we can be hope for others, and that we are not alone.

In chapter 17, Elijah meets a woman who has fallen on very tough times. Drought has afflicted the land, she is now a widow and raising a child on her own, and she is down to her last morsels of meal and oil to bake one final bit of bread before the two of them die of starvation. Elijah convinces her to take a leap of faith and surrender her last bit of food. And when she does, she discovers that God replenishes that jar of oil and jar of meal with enough—just enough—to make it through one day at a time.

Then in 1 Kings 18, after a fiery face-off between Elijah and the false prophets of Baal, Elijah takes his servant to a mountain and tells his servant to go up to the ridge and look off into the horizon to see if there was any sign of rain. He goes up and sees nothing. Elijah tells him to go up and look again, a second time, and a third time, and a fourth time. It is not until the seventh time that the servant says that he sees a small rain cloud, about the size of a human hand. Not much, but enough.

Now, what if Elijah or his servant had decided to give up at any time between the first and seventh time? The hope that God offers us requires our persistence—and our participation. God's hope is not something to sit back and wait for; it is something we step into and participate in.

And then in 1 Kings 19, my favorite story in the entire Old Testament, Elijah receives reassurance at the lowest point of his life and ministry. Queen Jezebel is furious that her prophets had been defeated on Mount

Carmel, and she issues a death sentence over Elijah's head. Elijah was running scared for his life and found himself in the middle of a wilderness. Exhausted. Bewildered. Alone. Distrustful. Skeptical. Angry. Finished.

And in that low point, God spoke to Elijah in a way that Elijah had never heard God speak before. God did not appear in a fire or wind or an earthquake, but came to Elijah as a still, small voice: "A sound. Thin. Quiet" (19:12). A whisper, just a bit louder than the noise within his heart, that he could only hear when he learned to silence every other voice but God's.

It was then that he could hear God give him the words he needed to hear. Words that reassured him he was not alone.

DAY 82   *1 Kings 12:1–16:34*

First Kings 16 is a rapid-fire review of the earliest kings of the divided kingdom, Israel in the north and Judah in the south. They had various resumes, but shared one common evaluation: Did they do "evil" or "right" in the sight of God? Ultimately, that's the only evaluation that matters. Is there any aspect of your life about which the same thing can be said?

DAY 83   *1 Kings 17:1–19:21*

The chapters of 1 Kings 17–19 are a treasure trove of encouragement for the weary and worn out. The widow's oil; the mountaintop face-off; the hand-sized cloud; the still, small voice: all reminders that whatever you are going through, God is in it with you.

DAY 84   *1 Kings 20:1–22:53*

Ahab was blind to the truth of Micaiah and blind to his envy of Naboth. It is fitting that he died wearing a disguise; he had deceived himself with his lies. How might you be open to the truths God and others have to reveal to you about yourself?

DAY 85   *2 Kings 1:1–8:15*

The stories of Elisha remind us that we can have hope in the hardest times. We need to keep pouring (as the widow did), stay humble (as Naaman learned), and open our eyes to God's presence (as the Arameans discovered).

DAY 86 *2 Kings 8:16–10:36*

What goes around, comes around. Ahab and Jezebel's descendant is assassinated in the land stolen from a man Ahab murdered. It is soon followed by Jezebel's death. "Don't judge, so that you won't be judged," Jesus says (Matthew 7:1). What goes around, comes around. What challenge does this truth pose for you?

DAY 87 *2 Kings 11:1–13:25*

Joash was a survivor of a murderous mother and cared about the upkeep of the Temple. But in the end, he, too, was unfaithful to God, and that's how he is remembered. In the end, faithfulness to God is what matters.

DAY 88   *2 Kings 14:1–17:41*

Even the good kings weren't perfect. Many of them still had a blind spot that caused their downfall and led people astray. May you adopt this prayer: God, help me discover my faults, no matter how small they first appear, and help me discover freedom in your grace.

NOTES & REFLECTIONS

2 Kings 18:1–1 Chronicles 27:34

Much of 1–2 Kings contains a refrain of warning: Israel and Judah and their kings must worship the Lord alone, observing the covenant God made with their ancestors, or ruin and destruction will come swiftly. In the final chapters of 2 Kings, the book drives toward the eventual conquest of Judah and Jerusalem by the Babylonians, as generations of disobedience and worship of other gods culminates in the predicted destruction. Hezekiah and Josiah are faithful kings, ceasing worship of other gods and centralizing worship in the Jerusalem Temple, but their obedience is not sufficient to offset the other rulers before and after them who broke God's covenant. Chapters 24 and 25 describe the final days of Judah, as the Babylonian Empire led by Nebuchadnezzar lays siege to Jerusalem, breaks into the city, tears down its walls, and burns the Temple along with "every important building" (25:9). The Babylonians captured Zedekiah, Judah's king, and brought him and most of Judah's people to Babylon.

The conquest of Jerusalem marks the beginning of the Babylonian Exile, one of the most decisive and theology-shaping events in the history of God's people. With the destruction of the Temple came the end of worship as the Israelites knew it, as sacrifices could no longer be offered. With the departure from the land came a disorientation—could they continue to be God's people outside the land God had given them, the land God promised to their ancestors? And with the capture of Judah's king, was the covenant God made with David of an everlasting dynasty now overturned? Could they continue worshipping, and if so, how? How would they maintain a sense of community with one another? What would their relationship with God be like going forward? Much of the Old Testament, especially 1–2 Kings and several of the prophetic books, wrestles with these questions.

The Exile ended around 539 BC, when Cyrus, King of Persia, conquered the Babylonians and made allowance for the people of Judah to return to their land. The books of 1–2 Chronicles retell the story of Israel from Genesis through the reign of Cyrus. Though the people eventually returned to Judah and Jerusalem, the Babylonian Exile left its mark on the Bible and on the imagination of our ancestors of faith. The questions they grappled with, and the practices and stories that guided them in Babylon, remained even after they returned. Through it all, one crucial conclusion emerged: God did not abandon them. Even in exile, God remained faithful to them.

DAY 89   *2 Kings 18:1–21:26*

The Assyrians engaged in psychological warfare against Judah, trying to turn the people against their king. But it didn't work. Hezekiah taught them not to engage impostors. May we also be strong to turn away threats to our devotion to God.

DAY 90   *2 Kings 22:1–25:30*

Josiah was the last good king of Judah. He rediscovered the law and removed the barriers that prevented people from following it. May we remove the obstacles that keep us from following, loving, and serving God.

DAY 91   *1 Chronicles 1:1–9:44*

These nine chapters recap the Old Testament so far, and remind us of the covenants with Abraham and David. As dysfunctional as our families might be, God can still do great things in and through them when we are faithful.

DAY 92   *1 Chronicles 10:1–12:40*

David realized his impulsiveness in asking for water that required his soldiers risking their lives. He honored them by offering the water to God. We need to control our impulses and make sure we honor those who provide for us.

DAY 93   *1 Chronicles 13:1–16:43*

What if your baptism is your "ark of the covenant," an outward and visible sign of God's covenant favor on your life? How will you preserve and cherish it, and live it out against injustice and evil today?

DAY 94   *1 Chronicles 17:1–22:1*

The site of the Temple was chosen at the intersection of penitence and praise, amid human suffering. Worship happens when you acknowledge your broken condition, confess your sins, and offer praise to God.

DAY 95   *1 Chronicles 22:2–27:34*

David prepared everything in place for Solomon to be able to build the Temple. Likewise, our primary job is often not to build the kingdom for ourselves, but to make it possible for the next generation to flourish in the faith.

NOTES & REFLECTIONS

1 Chronicles 28:1–2 Chronicles 24:27

The books of 1–2 Chronicles recap much of what we've read so far in Scripture, starting with Genesis and going to the reign of Cyrus of Persia, whose conquest of Babylon marked the end of the Babylonian Exile. These books were most likely written around 400–325 BC, when Judah and Jerusalem were under control of the Persian Empire.

First and Second Chronicles retell the story of Israel and Judah with specific emphases, leading to a different account in some respects from what we read in Genesis through 2 Kings. There is an emphasis on all Israel being united together in worship of God at the Jerusalem Temple, not just the Southern Kingdom of Judah. The books also highlight the connection between the Tabernacle built by Moses and the Temple built by Solomon, emphasizing the continuity of worship.

First Chronicles begins with genealogies tracing the descendants from Adam through the twelve tribes of Israel, down to those who returned from exile in Babylon (chapters 1–9), followed by an account of David's reign (chapters 10–28). Second Chronicles continues the narrative with Solomon's reign (chapters 1–9), followed by the history of Judah during the divided monarchy down through the Exile (chapters 10–36). Where 2 Kings ends with the destruction of Jerusalem and the deportation of its people to Babylon, 2 Chronicles ends with a decree from Cyrus, King of Persia who conquered Babylon in 539 BC. Cyrus declares that the people in exile may return to Jerusalem to build a temple to the Lord. This is where the books of Ezra and Nehemiah pick up, recounting the story of the return to Jerusalem and reconstruction of the Temple and the city's walls.

We may be tempted to wonder why the Old Testament contains two accounts of Israel's history: the one reflected in Genesis through 2 Kings, and a shorter version contained in 1–2 Chronicles. It's important to remember that the different writers, working in different contexts and from different perspectives, see differing aspects of God's relationship with the people. This is all the more true when we recognize that Genesis through 2 Kings was written by numerous authors across a period of several centuries. Two narratives provide a fuller account of God's activity among the Israelites and its meaning, in the same way that multiple camera angles give us a more complete picture of a scene we photograph.

DAY 96
1 Chronicles 28:1–29:30

Today's passage contains three lessons on stewardship: First, we give for the future to be built beyond us (28:8). Second, leaders give first as an example to all (29:6). And third, what we give is out of God's abundance to us (29:14). What difference do these principles make in our relationship to money, and how we give to God?

DAY 97
2 Chronicles 1:1–5:1

As in 1 Kings, we hear that the Temple was built in a partnership between Solomon and Hiram, Phoenician king of Tyre. It's a reminder of the good that can happen with interreligious cooperation.

DAY 98   *2 Chronicles 5:2–9:31*

Chronicles says nothing about Solomon's misdeeds recounted in 1 Kings, only his achievements. In the same way, we tend to focus on how good we are, rather than naming our shadows and confessing our sins. May we see ourselves with a balance that only comes from God's grace.

DAY 99   *2 Chronicles 10:1–13:22*

What are we to make of Rehoboam's response to Jeroboam? Is he to be criticized for not showing compassion, or commended for being principled? The reading invites reflection on the merits and limitations of compromise.

DAY 100   *2 Chronicles 14:1–16:14*

God's Spirit invites instability. It prompts change. When we welcome it, that's how we grow. It might make us fearful, but God says, "Be brave and don't lose heart, because your work will be rewarded!" (15:7).

DAY 101   *2 Chronicles 17:1–20:37*

Jehoshaphat instructed the leaders to govern with these three qualities: fear of the Lord, faithfulness, and wholehearted devotion (19:9 NRSV). These are good qualities to live by. How well do you live them out?

DAY 102   *2 Chronicles 21:1–24:27*

We read a story about an unsung hero, Jehoaida the prophet. He was willing to confront evil and take any risks necessary to carry out God's will. Because of him, Joash was protected and so was David's royal line. What can you learn from his example?

NOTES & REFLECTIONS

2 Chronicles 25:1–Nehemiah 4:23

The books of Ezra and Nehemiah relate how the people of Judah came back to Jerusalem after their time in exile in Babylon. They rebuilt the Temple, rebuilt the city walls, and reestablished themselves as a people in their own land.

For decades the people of Judah lived in captivity in Babylon. It was the single most traumatizing and consciousness-shaping event in the history of the Hebrew Bible. No event, including even slavery in Egypt, left more of a mark on the books of the Old Testament than the Babylonian Exile. More literature is devoted to describing the causes, the conditions, and the consequences of the Exile than any other experience in the Old Testament.

We read in Ezra and Nehemiah of how these exiled people of God undertook the daunting yet promising journey of return, bringing the Exile to an end and initiating a new chapter in the people's story. What would their return look like? Would it simply be a return to the way things were before, or would it be something else, something new? As we read these stories in Ezra and Nehemiah, it's good to keep in mind three key movements: Temple, Walls, and Heart.

It was the work of a man named Zerubbabel to rebuild the Temple, which had been reduced to rubble when the Babylonians destroyed Jerusalem. It was the work of Nehemiah to rebuild the walls around the city, which had likewise been brought down and stood in ruins ever since Nebuchadnezzar exiled the people to Babylon. Now, as you read their story, you come to realize that they were rebuilding more than just the brick and mortar of the walls around the city and the place of worship. Walls back then were not just a means of protection for a city's citizens. They were a symbol of identity for the people themselves. Those walls symbolized the kind of city that Jerusalem would believe itself to be. And the Temple was a reminder of God's closeness to the people, God's presence in their midst.

Ezra is important too, because his story reminds us that even more important than returning to worship, and returning to society, we need to decide about the human heart. The work of those returning from exile was rebuilding a people as much as it was rebuilding a Temple and a city's walls. Rebuilding the people was about character and integrity, and above all a commitment of their hearts to God and to the covenant God made with them. Walls, Temple, and Heart.

The reconstruction of the walls, Temple, and heart stood at the transition between the past and the future. After the Temple and the walls are rebuilt, Ezra creates a makeshift podium out of wood and reminds them of who God is and what God has called them to be. And as much as Ezra was calling people back to obedience to God, he was also calling them to be even better than they were before. When Ezra stood on that makeshift podium and read the Scriptures to the people, they shed tears. The Bible says there were two conflicting kinds of tears in that moment. Some people cried with joy. Others wept in grief. Two conflicting ideas, converging in that one moment at the threshold of the old and the new. Grief over what had been lost, and joy over what could be.

DAY 103   *2 Chronicles 25:1–28:27*

This long list of kings reinforces this continual point about the human condition. No one is perfect. Even the "good" ones have their flaws and make grievous errors. Holiness requires constant attentiveness and God's grace.

DAY 104   *2 Chronicles 29:1–32:33*

Hezekiah was one of the rare good kings in Judah. To be like him, we must preserve our worship of God, faithfully obey God, and seek God with all our heart (31:21).

DAY 105 $\qquad$ *2 Chronicles 33:1–36:23*

Today's reading contains a simple contrast: Manasseh or Josiah? The ruler who showed contempt for God's covenant and laws, or the one who sought to obey God wholeheartedly. Which one will I be more like today?

DAY 106 $\qquad$ *Ezra 1:1–3:13*

The Book of Ezra opens with the joyous return of the exiles and the rebuilding of the Temple. Paul said that our bodies are the "temple of the Holy Spirit" (1 Corinthians 6:19). In what ways is God wanting to do a rebuilding project on your life?

DAY 107
Ezra 4:1–6:22

Any work of building the kingdom of God will attract opposition. When those barriers arise, we need to be steadfast in our resolve, to boldly say, "We are the servants of the God of heaven and earth" (5:11). How might God be strengthening you to face opposition to the work you are doing for God's kingdom?

DAY 108
Ezra 7:1–10:44

Ezra's prayer not only offered confession for disobedience. It also motivated the people to remember who God is. Living by faith is not just getting our behaviors right. It is about being more attentive to what God is doing.

DAY 109   *Nehemiah 1:1–4:23*

Nehemiah prayed, then God called him to be the answer to his own prayer. He saw the devastation, and God called him to be the agent of restoration. That's sometimes what happens when we pray: God summons us to be the answer to our own prayers. How might you be the answer to your prayers for the world?

NOTES & REFLECTIONS

Nehemiah 5:1–Job 14:22

This week's readings bring the Book of Nehemiah to a close and move us through the Book of Esther. Esther stands apart in many ways from other writings in the Bible. There's even disagreement as to where it belongs in Scripture. In our Protestant Christian Bible, it's listed with the books of history: Kings, Chronicles, Ezra, Nehemiah, Esther. But in the Jewish Bible, it's listed among Ketuvim, the Writings, alongside books such as Lamentations and Ecclesiastes.

This is a clue to us that Esther is not a straightforward book. It's not really meant to tell us about actual events from the past with precise historical detail. Instead, it's meant to push us into discovering something new about how we live today. And it does so without many of the typical faith components that we come to depend on in every other book in the Bible. For example, there is not a single prayer lifted up by any character in the whole book, including Esther. There is not a single act of worship by any group of people. And then the big one: God is not mentioned once in the entire book. It is the only book in the entire Bible to not name God. Not even once.

But the lack of these overt faith elements teaches us to look for the hidden hand of God and the hidden faithfulness of the people in the story. We find both if we look carefully.

Esther exemplifies beauty and bravery, but in each case you have to look below the surface to see them. Make no mistake: Esther is described as a beautiful woman. But it was not simply her external beauty that was remarkable. It was her inner beauty. One rabbi commenting on Esther said that God gave her an "ingratiating kindness" that made her appear beautiful to everyone.

Esther's name likewise points to the hidden nature of her beauty. While the Persian meaning of Esther's name is *star*, the Hebrew root for the name "Esther" is the word *hidden*. A beauty that is hidden. She is a reminder to us that in every moment, no matter how odd or displaced we might feel, and no matter how absent God seems from you, God's beauty is there. Not always in obvious and bold ways, but in subtle and steady ways.

But Esther is not only known for her hidden beauty. She is also known for her bravery. In a time when her fellow Jews living in Persia were subject to sure genocide, Esther stepped up and forsook her own life for the well-being of others. She risked breaking royal law and the punishment of death by pleading her case before the king, and she said these words: "Even though it's against the law, I will go to the king; and if I am to die, then die I will" (4:16).

Esther's hidden beauty and her bravery, her quiet faithfulness to God, help us see how we might trust in God when God's ways are not always known and when the people around us don't share our faith.

In a different way, the Book of Job explores some of these same ideas, especially how we can know and trust God when things don't work out the way we expect them to.

DAY 110 *Nehemiah 5:1–7:73*

Nehemiah was not only rebuilding a wall, he had to rebuild economic justice between the rich and the poor, all while maintaining his own integrity and humility and overcoming threats from his enemies. He is one of the Old Testament's greatest leaders. What can you learn from his example?

DAY 111 *Nehemiah 8:1–10:39*

Returning from exile did not just involve rebuilding a wall. It meant building a consecrated people. Ezra's reforms rooted the people in the law and anchored them in confession, remembrance, commitment, and covenant renewal. How can you incorporate those four elements in your spiritual journey?

DAY 112 *Nehemiah 11:1–13:31*

Nehemiah finishes with some "spring cleaning": removal of impurities from the Temple and ungodliness from the people, and a return to Sabbath keeping. The wall may have defined their city, but only faithfulness would define their hearts. How might you do some "spring cleaning" in your soul today?

DAY 113 *Esther 1:1–4:17*

God is not named in Esther, but God is active. God's work toward justice will not be deterred, whether we choose to participate in it or not (4:14). We have been called "for a moment like this." How can you participate in God's work today?

DAY 114 *Esther 5:1–10:3*

Haman is killed by the very device with which he intended to kill Mordecai. It's a plot twist that is a commentary on sin. We are undone by how we would undo others. It's a corollary of the Golden Rule that highlights "just deserts": you will have done to you what you would do unto others.

DAY 115 *Job 1:1–5:27*

The story of Job upends much of what the Bible has said so far about rewarding only the faithful and punishing only the wicked. It allows us to ask, Why, God? The permission to ask that question is itself liberating. In what ways might you be asking that question of God today?

DAY 116

Job 6:1–14:22

Job's prayer is raw, honest, and real. It gives us permission to do the same when we are struggling with the faith and with God. Can you believe that God can handle your lament, impatience, doubt, and fear?

NOTES & REFLECTIONS

Job 15:1–Psalm 12:8

This week we conclude the Book of Job and begin reading the Psalms. Job is a book of Wisdom Literature, a genre that deals with traditions of wisdom and how to live well as human beings. While much Wisdom Literature emphasizes a principle of getting what you deserve—the righteous will be rewarded, and the wicked will be punished—Job reckons with the harsh truth that reality doesn't always work out this way. Where is God, and what is God up to, when a righteous man like Job suffers for no apparent reason? Much of Job is a dialogue in which Job and his friends wrestle with this question, and even when God speaks at the end it doesn't leave us with ready-made answers. Job highlights the mystery of God's ways and the struggle to remain faithful when we can't see everything.

The Book of Psalms is the songbook of ancient Israel and Judah: the collection of songs and poems in a variety of forms, for a variety of settings, both individual and communal, that gave God's people a way to join together and name what was in their hearts. They represent hundreds of years of worship, prayer, celebration, thanksgiving, and lament. The current collection of 150 Psalms is organized into five books, echoing the five books of the Torah, with each book ending with a short hymn of praise to God:

Book 1: Psalms 1–41
Book 2: Psalms 42–72
Book 3: Psalms 73–89
Book 4: Psalms 90–106
Book 5: Psalms 107–150

When we read the Psalms, we find every emotion represented. Love, praise, joy, grief, awe, thanksgiving, sadness. They are all there, reminding us that all our emotions are God-given and can help us express and live our faith. Even anger is there, represented in what are known as imprecatory psalms, such as Psalm 7:6:

> Get up, Lord; get angry!
>> Stand up against the fury of my foes!
> Wake up, my God;
>> you command that justice be done!

There are passages like this all throughout the Psalms, passages that name other people as our evil enemies, passages that ask God to smite them and punish them. We are right to be troubled by these words. But the presence of these psalms in our Bible remind us of the fact that this kind of vengeance-seeking anger is, in fact, in our hearts, whether we like it or not. And when we ask, What are we supposed to do with these Scriptures? God is actually prompting us to ask the questions, Why is this feeling in our hearts to begin with? And more importantly, What are we supposed to do with it? The Psalms help us give these emotions, even anger, over to God.

As you read the psalms every day over the next several weeks, let them speak to you. Let them speak on your behalf. And most of all, let them draw you closer to God and to one another so that we can come to same conclusion as the author of Psalm 7:17:

> I will thank the Lord
>> for his righteousness;
> I will sing praises
>> to the name of the Lord Most High.

DAY 117
Job 15:1–21:34

Even Job's friends are against him, speaking more than listening, telling him it's his fault, and urging him to shake off the pain. They are unhelpful, and Job feels alone. Job 17 is as honest a look at the human condition as there is in the whole Bible. How might you befriend someone in need in a more helpful way than Job's friends do?

DAY 118
Job 22:1–31:40

Job asserts his integrity. Everything was going wrong in his life, but he could still know that he was obeying God's laws the best he could. Our integrity might be all we have left, but that is enough. It's often the one thing we can control.

DAY 119 *Job 32:1–37:24*

Elihu offers what Job's three friends do not: a reminder of who God is. Job and his friends focused on Job's actions and qualities, looking for causes to his suffering. Elihu pointed to God, to remind them of God's goodness, mercy, and might. What difference does Elihu's words make in your times of suffering?

DAY 120 *Job 38:1–42:17*

God shows up to remind Job that he is not God. Amid suffering or change, we remember that we are not God; nor do we have to be. The implicit response to everything in this last reading is, Only God can. And that is good news for us.

DAY 121

Psalms 1:1–4:8

Our enemies don't have to always be other people. They can be sadness, fear, loneliness, grief, and anxiety. The Psalms say that God is there to preserve us at all times from those enemies. That promise is ours to claim. What "enemies" are you facing today?

DAY 122

Psalms 5:1–8:9

Psalm 6 is for anyone struggling beyond words, weeping beyond tears, and longing for God to show up. It's a psalm for the nighttime of the soul. It offers no false hope. It only offers this: God is listening, and that is all you need. Is that enough for you?

DAY 123

Psalms 9:1–12:8

The Psalms make it clear that God is always on the side of the oppressed. This raises the question, How am I the oppressor? Or to what degree am I only thinking that I am oppressed, in order to curry favor from God?

NOTES & REFLECTIONS

Psalm 13:1–41:13

Whenever we read the Psalms, whether it's an individual's song or that of a group, the setting is important—the setting in which the psalm was first heard and used, as well as the setting in which we encounter it right now, and everything in-between.

Psalm 23, for example, is one of the most beloved and well-known biblical passages in history. And like many, even most, of the Psalms, Psalm 23 has sounded different depending on where and in what situation it was recited or heard.

How does it sound to you when you hear it in church, in a worship service?

How do you suppose it sounded to early Jews who heard it sung for the first time in the Temple?

And how do you think it sounds to a family at a graveside, hearing it from their loved one's Bible?

What does it sound like when a soldier recites it from memory while clutching his dog tag?

Or when a young couple reads it on a wall hanging in their brand-new nursery?

The setting in which we read Psalm 23 helps us hear in it different resonances. It's also interesting that the setting is one of the first things we notice in the words of this psalm. We don't know who the actual author of it was—some say David, but we don't know for sure. Whoever the author was, it must have been a landscape artist or a cinematographer. Restful waters. Grassy pastures. Darkest valleys. Set aside the verbs and proper nouns for a minute, and it's as if Psalm 23 were a series of paintings, one landscape after another.

So this poem, like many of the Psalms, beckons you first of all to pay attention to your current setting: How would you define your darkest valley right now? What does it look like? What are your enemies? Who are they?

But more importantly, where are your restful waters right now and your grassy pastures that God is letting you rest in? the blessed settings that God is giving you right now that you might not be noticing?

Notice also the way this psalm speaks of God, always in the present tense. The Lord is my shepherd. God lets me rest. God keeps me alive. God guides me. God sets a table.

Nowhere in this psalm does God act in the future or the past tense. This is not about something God will do, or something God has done in the past. Other psalms talk about God's record and God's promise, to be fulfilled in the future, and still others recount God's acts in the past. But Psalm 23 is about God in the present moment—what God is doing right now.

So many of the Psalms invite us to pay attention to the present, opening ourselves to God in the moment that is before us. May you read them in that spirit this week.

DAY 124   *Psalms 13:1–16:11*

There cannot be rebirth without lament. Lament honors life and takes love and truth seriously. It acknowledges loss, so that we can then trust in God's faithful love into the future. In what ways are you lamenting today?

DAY 125   *Psalms 17:1–20:9*

A connecting thread among all the psalms in today's reading is the grateful recognition that everything one has in life is a gift from God. Every achievement, possession, and experience comes from a generous, loving God. How is that true in your life? How will you express your gratitude to God today?

DAY 126   *Psalms 21:1–24:10*

Before the classic Psalm 23, there is Psalm 22, a psalm of longing and suffering. Sometimes you have to go through the longing before you can get to assurance. And it's followed by Psalm 24, in which one enters the glorious presence of God.

DAY 127   *Psalms 25:1–28:9*

The psalmist consistently remembers that we are not self-sufficient. We need God for everything. To conquer our inner turmoil, to make peace with our enemies, and to overcome sin all require God's presence and action. This requires humility, repentance, and a desire to follow God.

DAY 128   *Psalms 29:1–32:11*

Many psalms hold two ideas in tension: I am lost and hurting; God is faithful and is with me. It is possible to experience both the dark and the light, for each outlines the other. "God, where are you?" is met with "God is always here."

DAY 129   *Psalms 33:1–36:12*

Psalm 34 shows David's heart as he faked being out of his mind in order to hide his true identity from others. Despite the outward roles you play for others to see, what is in your heart? Does your heart trust and praise God, or is it turned inward upon yourself?

DAY 130   *Psalms 37:1–41:13*

Humility ties these texts together. We are called to trust (Psalm 37), repent (Psalm 38), embrace life's brevity (Psalm 39), wait patiently (Psalm 40), and care for the poor (Psalm 41). How well is humility expressed in your life in these areas?

NOTES & REFLECTIONS

Psalm 42:1–68:35

In many of the psalms, we discover the comfort and strength we need to make it through the day. But then there are other psalms, like Psalm 51, that stop us in our tracks and push us to look at things inside ourselves that we would much rather ignore.

It is the power of Scriptures like these to move us to confession. To push the darker truths within us to light. And while we may not like it, this is a deeply important thing for us to do.

Psalm 51 is also one of the psalms linked to a specific event related elsewhere in the Bible. A note introducing the psalm comes from David, "when the prophet Nathan came to him just after he had been with Bathsheba." We know the story from 2 Samuel 11, in which David sleeps with Bathsheba and has her husband, Uriah, killed to cover it up. The shock of it all is not just that there was adultery and murder. The shock is that the great King David, the one who is glorified above them all, committed some of the most harmful and violent sins in the whole Bible. It is the Bible's way of saying that none of us—not even the most pious appearing among us—is impervious to sin.

This psalm invites you to a preemptive confessional: to come clean before God and others, before your sins come to light.

And you might even use these words as a template for your own confession: God, I know my sins. Have mercy on me. Wash me. Cleanse me. Create a new heart in me.

Whenever you see the word *heart* in the Bible, remember that the ancient world understood the heart as encompassing the whole of a person's being. David did not just ask for a change in his feelings or emotions, but a complete reboot of his values, his perspective, and his behavior. David said to God, "You desire truth in the inward being; / therefore teach me wisdom in my secret heart" (51:6 NRSV).

And I think this is why David is more highly regarded than Saul and Solomon, and every other king, even though he did some things that were worse than what they did. Because of Psalm 51. It's not just that David confessed his sins, God graciously forgave him and helped him to make things right.

You see, that's the thing about confession. It's painful. It's necessary. But it's also liberating. Because it reminds you that you are not as powerful and in control as you think. And there is freedom in that. I think that's why Psalm 51, for all of its sober and solemn confession, ends in such a beautiful and glorious way, starting in verse 15: "Lord, open my lips, / and my mouth will proclaim your praise."

God does not leave us to wallow in our sin and bathe in the afterglow of our worst mistakes. God indeed cleanses us with hyssop and creates a new heart in us, and the only response that is worthy of such a gift is praise, gratitude, and thanksgiving. The Psalms help us to recognize that and claim it for our own faith.

DAY 131 *Psalms 42:1–45:17*

Psalm 42 reveals the heart at its most honest and vulnerable. It gives us permission to acknowledge our downcast soul, our doubts, and the pressures of those who don't believe in God. But it never gives up hope. What meaning does Psalm 42 bring you today?

DAY 132 *Psalms 46:1–49:20*

Today's psalms make quite a sound: mountains shaking, waters roaring, people praising, God shouting, labor pains, spoken wisdom. But amid the noise is this command: "Be still, and know I am God" (46:10 NRSV). How well are you hearing God amid the noise of your life?

DAY 133 *Psalms 50:1–53:6*

Right actions are not enough. We must do them out of a "clean heart," from penitence, humility, and a seeking after God. The alternative is the way of the fool, who says there is no God. How will you orient your heart Godward today, rather than inward?

DAY 134 *Psalms 54:1–56:13*

"Cast your burden on the LORD" (55:22) means that God not only can carry your burden (cast your burden ON the Lord); God can also carry you (and God will support you). God is strong enough to do both, so we need to "release" ourselves to God and "receive" the love and power of God.

DAY 135 *Psalms 57:1–59:17*

The psalmist does not pray for the death of his enemies, only that they will suffer the consequences of their own sin (59:11-13). The worst punishment we often experience is the consequences of our own sins and the wrong choices we make.

DAY 136 *Psalms 60:1–63:11*

The image of the rock is a recurring one in these readings. It is an image of strength and stability, which only God can provide. Amid change, instability, and uncertainty, how might you depend on God to be led to a rock "higher than I"(61:2)?

DAY 137 *Psalms 64:1–68:35*

There are many images of nature in today's psalms, reminding us that God is evident all around us (seas, rain, mountains, clouds). Whenever you feel alone, you can just open your eyes, breathe in the Spirit, and enjoy God's presence around you.

NOTES & REFLECTIONS

Psalm 69:1–101:8

Many of the psalms call us to praise and thanksgiving, and a number of these had their origin in the worship of the Israelites in Jerusalem. Psalm 100 is an example. When you read Psalm 100, you can't help but imagine what it must have been like for those Israelites, shouting and cheering as they ascended the hill toward Jerusalem, with the mighty gates of the city looming larger in their sights.

The psalm says, "Enter his gates with thanks; / enter his courtyards with praise!" (v. 4).

Of the many Hebrew words for praise, one of the more frequent is *halal*, from which we get the word *Hallelujah* meaning "Praise the Lord." Used here it envisions a bold, public act of praise: "Shout triumphantly" (v. 1), serving with celebration and cries of joy. It calls to mind the behavior of David when the ark of the covenant entered Jerusalem, when the king danced and made a fool of himself without caring what others thought.

It's the kind of praise we do in sports stadiums or theaters or at rock concerts. Psalms like Psalm 100 invite us to engage in this kind of praise as an act of worship—loud, joyous, public praise and thanksgiving to God.

Psalm 100 does not tell us to make a joyful noise to the Lord only when we feel like it. It does not say, "Serve the LORD with celebration!" (v. 2), just when all is well or convenient or meets our usual expectations. The call to praise is constant. Even and especially when we don't feel like it.

And the good news is that Psalm 100 not only tells us that praise and thanksgiving are important, it also shows us how to do it.

The verse does make a very subtle but important distinction between praise and thanksgiving. We often lump them together, and they are both important. Just as a song is made up of both lyric and melody, you can't have praise without thanksgiving. And vice versa.

But here's the distinction that I invite you think about: Thanksgiving focuses on what God has given you, and praise focuses on who God is. Thanksgiving is about the gift. Praise is about the giver. Thanksgiving shows gratitude for the gift itself; praise is gratitude for the character of the giver. I think it's easier to practice thanksgiving. To count your blessings, to remember the good things that God has given you. But that is just the place to start. It is not the finish line. Eventually, we must move from entering the gates with thanks to moving into the courtyards with praise.

Praise is acknowledging God's goodness, power, and love, regardless of our situations, regardless of whether we feel blessed or not. Praise simply means, God, I am in awe of you. Just being in your presence is breathtaking. And regardless of what is happening in me and around me, there is no better place to be but in your presence.

Many of the psalms help us understand what it means to praise God and give us words and emotions to guide us in doing so. These lyrical expressions of our faith call us not just to give thanks for what we receive, but for the God who gives them.

DAY 138 *Psalms 69:1–72:20*

The final psalm of David is a prayer for his son Solomon and his rule over the kingdom. It's a good reminder that our prayers should not all be about ourselves, but for future generations, and for God's grace to be revealed through them.

DAY 139 *Psalms 73:1–75:10*

When the days seem long and the nights seem dark, the psalmist affirms that the presence of God alone is all that matters. "My body and my heart fail, / but God is my heart's rock and my share forever (73:26). What difference do these words make in your life today?

DAY 140 *Psalms 76:1–78:72*

Psalm 77 is helpful to read when your soul is troubled, your nights are sleepless, and you are reaching for God in the dark. The first half (vv. 1-10) names the stirring. The second half (vv. 11-20) invokes God's power and presence. Both are necessary.

DAY 141 *Psalms 79:1–84:12*

Psalm 84 is a song of a content soul that has found refuge in the presence of God. It meant the Temple, but could mean for us any condition in which we feel assured that God is with us. To feel that joy and strength is the chief aim of life. How will you find refuge and contentment in God today?

DAY 142   *Psalms 85:1–89:52*

Psalms 88 and 89 couldn't be more different, but both coincide in the Christian life. Prayers of despondency (Psalm 88) and praise (Psalm 89) aren't contradictory or mutually exclusive. Each allows for the existence of the other; both are necessary. How do you experience both today?

DAY 143   *Psalms 90:1–95:11*

We are not alive forever. That thought is scary, but it is also liberating. Savor each moment, but don't grip it too tightly. Let the river of life carry you, rather than trying to control it. Feel God's presence, power, and protection, and give thanks often.

DAY 144

Psalms 96:1–101:8

Praise (Psalm 96–100) and integrity (Psalm 101) go hand in hand. If we orient our spirit in praise to God, we discover the standard with which we are to live. And if we live a life of integrity, we learn to give thanks for God's power and strength. How will you live with praise and integrity today?

NOTES & REFLECTIONS

Psalm 102:1–126:6

As you've no doubt realized by now, there are a number of different types of psalms. Some represent an individual or a community asking God for help, while others offer praise and others express thanksgiving or trust in God. Still others have a liturgical background, evidently used in specific worship settings, while others focus on Judah's king or on Jerusalem.

One kind of psalm is a historical psalm, which recounts important events in the history of Israel and Judah, usually with an emphasis on God's presence and action. Psalms 105 and 106 are examples of historical psalms. Psalm 105 calls for the people to praise God, reciting God's mighty actions in the past as reasons for praise: "Sing to God; / sing praises to the Lord; / dwell on all his wondrous works!" (105:2). The psalm recalls the covenant with Abraham and Jacob, the story of Joseph, and how Moses and Aaron led the Israelites out of slavery in Egypt. It describes the plagues on Egypt, God's guidance of the people through the wilderness, and God's provision of water, quail, and food from heaven.

Psalm 106 continues the narrative, beginning again with an invitation to praise God before turning to Israel's experiences in the wilderness. Here, though, the focus shifts from God's mighty actions to Israel's rebellion and sin, and God's faithfulness to Israel. It ends with a plea for God to save the people, from the perspective of captivity and exile: "LORD our God, save us!" (106:47). Most biblical scholars conclude that Psalms 105 and 106 are meant to go together, representing a continuous historical narrative that describes both God's wondrous works and the people's rebellion. Other examples of historical psalms are Psalm 78 and Psalm 136.

Psalms 105 and 106 are also concerned with praising God, confessing the people's sins, and asking God for deliverance, elements from other types of psalms. This leads some scholars to identify them as a hymn of praise. In fact, some of the psalms can be a challenge to categorize for precisely this reason; they often combine aspects of several different kinds, in a variety of ways and for different purposes. The historical psalms in particular recount the past not for its own sake, but for a larger purpose: to motivate praise of God, to teach the people, or to express thanks for what God has done.

DAY 145 *Psalms 102:1–104:35*

These psalms draw a contrast between our finite mortality and the everlasting grandeur of God. Remember that whatever sags your soul is temporary. Once you are drawn into an awareness of God's mighty love and power, all your troubles will seem small and temporary.

DAY 146 *Psalms 105:1–107:43*

There are four stories of people who need God in Psalm 107: those experiencing desert, darkness, sinfulness, and storms. In each instance, we can give thanks, for God shows steadfast love and wonderful works. Which of those stories resonates with you today?

DAY 147

Psalms 108:1–112:10

Psalm 112 returns to the themes in Psalm 1. The blessed life follows God's commandments, does justice, cares for the poor, is generous, lives without fear, and has a steady heart. The wicked life is the opposite. Choose the blessed life.

DAY 148

Psalms 113:1–118:29

These psalms today remind us that in times of distress, we can find in God refuge and strength (Psalm 118) as well as rest (Psalm 116). Even when others (or even when we) question the existence of God, "[God's] faithful love lasts forever" (118:29). Feel God's presence, power, and protection, and give thanks often.

DAY 149 *Psalm 119:1-88*

The words *heart, soul, lips, eyes,* and *mouth* are recurring throughout Psalm 119. It's a reminder that following God should involve our whole being. Not just our minds, but our whole selves.

DAY 150 *Psalm 119:89-176*

Psalm 119 reminds us that reading the Scriptures, particularly its commands, need not be dreary or threatening. It can also be a gateway to joy, life, and contentment if we bring to it a spirit of expectation. How will you live with that kind of expectation today?

DAY 151   *Psalms 120:1–126:6*

These psalms were sung as worshippers ascended the Temple mount. They prepared themselves for worship with prayers for deliverance and assurance, and shouts of praise. How might God's people prepare for worship in that way today?

NOTES & REFLECTIONS

Psalm 127:1–Proverbs 3:35

In this week's readings we conclude the Book of Psalms and begin the Book of Proverbs. The Book of Proverbs is a collection of sayings, many but not all of which are attributed to King Solomon (see Proverbs 1:1; 10:1; 25:1). Proverbs 25 describes "the men of Hezekiah" copying or collecting the proverbs of Solomon. Hezekiah was king of Judah during the late eighth and early seventh century BC, more than two hundred years after Solomon's reign. Certain proverbs are attributed to men named Agur and Lemuel (Proverbs 30:1; 31:1), while others are simply described as "words of the wise" (22:17). Proverbs is the work of many different authors and compilers over a long period of time, associated both with Judah's kings and with ancient Near Eastern wisdom traditions.

The books of Proverbs, Ecclesiastes, and Job are examples of Wisdom Literature in the Bible. Wisdom Literature refers to a genre of writing from the ancient Near East that concerns itself with wisdom and virtue—how to live rightly and well—written by sages or teachers. Examples of Wisdom Literature exist among ancient Egyptian and Mesopotamian writings, helping biblical scholars better understand this genre of literature. In addition to the books of Proverbs, Ecclesiastes, and Job, some psalms are examples of Wisdom Literature in the Bible.

The books of Wisdom Literature have a different quality from many of the other books of the Old Testament. They don't touch upon the main narrative tracing the story of Israel and Judah and their ancestors, like we see in the Pentateuch and Historical Books and Prophets. Wisdom Literature instead deals with more universal aspects of the human condition, with advice, instruction, and observation pertaining to everyday experience and the things that most people encounter over the course of their lives.

While much of the other literature in the Bible describes God in the history of the Israelite people, Wisdom Literature concerns itself with the values that hold true throughout the story: right understanding, virtue, character, courage, integrity. The books of wisdom help us see what it means to have a life characterized by these values and how we can cultivate such positive and life-giving qualities in our daily practices and inner attitudes.

As you read through the books of Proverbs and Ecclesiastes over the next few weeks, may you find them to be a source of wisdom and guidance for your own life. May you hear their exhortation about the value of wisdom, the beginning of which is fear of God and a fundamental orientation toward the Creator of all things. And may you find within them God's own Word, speaking to you exactly what you need to hear in this moment.

DAY 152 *Psalms 127:1–130:8*

The Psalms remind us to trust, wait, hope, and long for God, when we don't know how things will turn out (Psalm 130). But they also remind us of what we can do: build our efforts and our hearts on God's desires (Psalms 127–128). How will you do those things today?

DAY 153 *Psalms 131:1–136:26*

Too often our praise of God is more about us than it is about God, about what God has done for us and to us. These psalms (especially Psalms 135–146) remind us how to praise God simply for who God is: God's power, love, greatness, and work throughout history. How will you praise God in a less egocentric way today?

DAY 154   *Psalms 137:1–140:13*

Psalm 137 is from the lowest point in Israelite history (the Exile), and it is followed by Psalm 138 remembering the highest point (David, Zion). Life has highs and lows, sometimes back to back, but what doesn't change is God's faithful presence and awareness (Psalm 139). Whether you are in a "high" or "low" right now, how will you experience God's faithfulness today?

DAY 155   *Psalms 141:1–144:15*

We all have enemies. Some are external, most are internal. The psalmists often pray for their enemies to be destroyed, but these readings are prayers for us to be preserved and protected against them. Our enemies won't always be defeated, but God helps us endure them. How might you pray for that kind of endurance today?

DAY 156

Psalms 145:1–150:6

A life of praise anchored in God's grace is the only song that matters, the *cantus firmus* ("fixed melody") according to theologian Dietrich Bonhoeffer. Everything else in your life is just harmony. How will you sing a song of praise to God in your life today?

DAY 157

Proverbs 1:1–2:22

There is such a thin line between being God-fearing and walking the way of evil. The opening of Proverbs reminds us that it is only in seeking wisdom outside us (from God) rather than trusting in oneself alone that we can be faithful.

DAY 158 *Proverbs 3:1-35*

It's not about you. It's not about the wisdom you gain, or the capacity you have to decide what's best. It is about trusting in God's wisdom both in the moment and in the long haul, so that your path will become straight.

NOTES & REFLECTIONS

Proverbs 4:1–15:33

Proverbs 10 begins a section of the book that contains many short sayings, distinct from the longer meditations found in much of Proverbs 1–9. One technique found in these short sayings is antithetic parallelism, in which the second part of a statement contrasts with the first. We find numerous examples of these in Proverbs 12:

> The wicked are trapped
>> by the transgressions of their lips,
>> but the righteous escape from distress (v. 13).

> Fools see their own way as right,
>> but the wise listen to advice (v. 15).

> Some chatter on like a stabbing sword,
>> but a wise tongue heals (v. 18).

These two-line sayings contrast the ways of the foolish or wicked with the ways of the wise or righteous. The resulting statements are effective, clear, and memorable. One of the reasons to love the Wisdom Literature is that the sages don't mince words. There is nothing mysterious about the observations they make or truths they declare with these sayings. These statements understand us. They tell it to us straight. The Book of Proverbs is filled with passages like these; they give us practical ways to live life as God intends, and to avoid the ways of sin and harm.

These proverbs aren't exactly comparing two different kinds of people. Rather, they are helping us discern wise and foolish behavior. They are describing the wisdom and foolishness, the righteousness and wickedness, within each one of us and the opportunities to exercise either one in the choices we make.

Imagine persons who are so focused on accumulating knowledge that they become ignorant of how to relate to others. The wise become foolish.

Or persons that are so obsessed with reputation and success that they turn into a failure in their family. Or persons that are so focused on living a healthy lifestyle that they develop an unhealthy sense of control and self-judgment. In these examples, it's easy for us to see that wisdom and foolishness can coexist within our hearts and minds, as can righteousness and wickedness. Not that we need these examples; we know it quite well from our own experience.

That's what Proverbs illustrates for us through its contrastive statements. Proverbs cautions us to beware wickedness and foolishness, and to pursue wisdom and righteousness, because both ways are in our hearts and both paths lie before us. These sayings help us see the paths more clearly and recognize righteousness and wickedness for what they are, but it is up to us to choose which path we will follow.

DAY 159

Proverbs 4:1–5:23

There is no quicker way to "utter ruin" than our unwillingness to hear hard truths about ourselves or to refuse to be corrected. Openness to critique is a discipline that draws the line between wisdom and wickedness (5:11-14). How might you be more open to helpful critique?

DAY 160

Proverbs 6:1–7:27

Proverbs 6:16-19 names seven abominable sins. Considering and living out their opposites constitute the best way to live: humility, truthfulness, self-sacrifice, love, discipline, integrity, and peace making. What will you do to incorporate these virtues into your life?

DAY 161 *Proverbs 8:1–9:18*

In these Proverbs, God's wisdom is personified as a person you should get to know. So just like starting any other relationship, getting to know God's wisdom requires being attentive, humble, eager to be in its presence and willing to be vulnerable and real. How can you get to know God better today?

DAY 162 *Proverbs 10:1–11:31*

Proverbs 10 starts the book's "good vs. bad" section: each verse is a Do vs. Don't. It reminds us that the righteous life is a constant choice to honor God and not to honor self. A good example is from verse 12: "Hate stirs up conflict, / but love covers all offenses." Which of the "don't" qualities do you need to work on?

DAY 163　　　　*Proverbs 12:1–13:25*

Proverbs 12:16-26 is a master class on the power of speech. Words can do great harm, but they can also bring healing (v. 18), joy (v. 20), favor (v. 22), encouragement for the anxious (v. 25), and guidance (v. 26). How can your words be less like a sword and more like a salve (v. 18)?

DAY 164　　　　*Proverbs 14:1-35*

Integrity signifies fear of God, but "a crooked path" disregards God. In other words: guard the emotions no one else can see, and do good even if no one else is watching. How can you strive to live with integrity, and how can the wisdom of Proverbs help you?

DAY 165

Proverbs 15:1-33

Proverbs 15 has seven practical insights for daily life: Don't be lazy, watch your words, be open to correction, don't be boastful, be slow to anger, be of good cheer. But most important: love is all that matters. How might you go "seven-for-seven" today?

NOTES & REFLECTIONS

Proverbs 16:1–26:28

Reading from Proverbs can feel like drinking from a fire hose. I'm not sure who first coined the phrase, "drinking from a fire hose," but it's a memorable enough line that it certainly came to mind one day as I was reading these Scriptures.

That's the power of a pithy, memorable phrase. It doesn't matter where it came from or the original context behind it. It doesn't matter what the phrase "drinking from a fire hose" was originally intended to mean. What I know is that in this case, in this particular context, it's true.

We have to read Proverbs in a way that is very different from the way we read just about every other scripture in the Bible. Often, when we read other texts, we are attuned to asking certain automatic questions: What is the backstory? Who is the audience? What's happened before this point, and what comes after it?

The thing about Proverbs is, it has none of those answers. That's what makes some of them harder to understand than other things we read. But that's also what makes them so powerful and so applicable. Especially right now, for you and me. Because here's the deal. Unlike other Bible verses, where we look for the backstory in order to discover the truth in that verse, Proverbs flips that around. We take the truth, and we become the story that lives out that truth.

Here's an example. I constantly give thanks for my dad. To this day he is a constant source of wisdom and guidance for me. One of the phrases he taught me early in my childhood is, Think first.

I don't remember when he first told me that line. I couldn't tell you if he said it to me after I accidentally put a crack in the drywall or touched a hot stove or put a dent in the car. All of those things happened, by the way. But it doesn't matter the exact situation in which my dad first told me to think first. All I know is, I haven't forgotten it.

Think before you speak. Think before you act. Consider the consequences. Because if you don't, that's when bad things happen. It's the wisdom of that phrase, not the backstory of it that sticks with me to this day.

I think that's how we are meant to approach Proverbs. In a podcast interview, Dr. Anne Stewart of Princeton Theological Seminary shared some helpful advice with the people of Hyde Park United Methodist Church in Tampa on how to read the Proverbs. She suggested that we don't try to read them in large batches, in one gulp setting. Rather, we should take our time with them. Read them slowly. Ponder and savor their meaning. Sip them and, in many cases, find the one Proverb—just one— that speaks to each of us on any particular day.

DAY 166 *Proverbs 16:1-33*

Pride, arrogance, haughtiness, and a boastful spirit are denounced throughout Proverbs. It's the opposite of a wise life, "an abomination to the LORD" (16:5 NRSV) and a precursor to destruction (16:18). Do a self-check today. How are you thinking too highly of yourself?

DAY 167 *Proverbs 17:1–18:24*

Proverbs 17–18 has so many choice nuggets of wisdom: Forgiveness (17:9 NRSV), A joyful heart (17:22), Friendship (18:24). One to pay particular attention to is about empathy: "Fools find no pleasure in understanding, / but only in expressing their opinion" (18:2). How can you better cultivate empathy in your relationships with others, particularly with those with whom you disagree?

DAY 168

Proverbs 19:1–20:30

Proverbs 19–20 reminds us of two key aspects of the good life: integrity and loyalty. Integrity is what you do when no one else is watching (19:1; 20:7 NRSV). Loyalty is what you do when everyone else depends on you (19:22; 20:6 NRSV). How will you strengthen both qualities today?

DAY 169

Proverbs 21:1–22:29

Proverbs 22:1-4 offers the antidote to greed. "A good reputation is better than much wealth.... The reward of humility and the fear of the LORD / is wealth, honor, and life." Being honorable and humble, that is greater than riches and rewards.

DAY 170 *Proverbs 23:1-35*

Proverbs 23 is a warning against two prominent temptations: 1) the allure of riches, and 2) the allure of gluttony and drunkenness. Staying content, clean, and sober is a key to the wise life. How strong are those temptations in your life, and what will you do about it?

DAY 171 *Proverbs 24:1-34*

Proverbs 24 reminds us of the power of speech. We should be unafraid to speak hard truths to people who need to hear it (vv. 23-26) and refrain from speaking falsehoods about people, even if we feel they deserve it (vv. 28-29). How will you harness your speech for good, rather than for ill?

DAY 172

Proverbs 25:1–26:28

Proverbs 26 denounces laziness (vv. 13-16) and stirring up strife (vv. 17-28), suggesting the two are related. It's a reminder that empathy, peacemaking, speaking truth lovingly, and handling conflict in a healthy way are hard work. Anything less is laziness.

NOTES & REFLECTIONS

Proverbs 27:1–Ecclesiastes 12:14

Ecclesiastes, like Proverbs and Job, is an example of Wisdom Literature in the Bible. Recall that Wisdom Literature concerns itself with the teachings of the wise and with how to live rightly in the world that God has created. In Proverbs we see contrasts between the behavior of the righteous and the wicked, the wise and the foolish, with a corresponding exhortation to choose the way of wisdom and righteousness. Underlying that advice is the idea that righteousness and wisdom are the better way and the closely related idea that this way will be rewarded while the way of wickedness and foolishness leads to ruin.

Ecclesiastes, however, presents a different picture of the world—one where the righteous aren't always rewarded, where wicked people sometimes seem to prosper, where the fastest runner doesn't always win the race or the strongest fighter win the battle, because "accidents can happen to anyone" (9:11). In this world the same fate can happen to all, and it seems to matter little in the end whether one behaves well or badly.

Ecclesiastes presents an outlook that some would call pessimistic, and others realistic. It's based on observation of the world as it is, and it acknowledges the fact that life really doesn't always work out as we want. Ecclesiastes presents life as it is, unvarnished, in order to give us permission to name just how frail and fragile life is right now.

Sure, Ecclesiastes does not easily lend itself to hope and promise. And that's okay. Ecclesiastes is just part of the Bible; it's not the entire Bible. And we can turn to other books for good news and hope and promise. But as any good doctor would tell you, you can't have the right prescription without a proper diagnosis. You can't have healing without acknowledging the pain. As one of my theology professors loved to say to us students, "If Jesus is the answer, what was the question?"

That is one reason I love Ecclesiastes. It is unafraid to name the hard questions, and it challenges us to think about spiritual matters beyond easy answers and simple clichés. The Teacher of Ecclesiastes says it like it is and serves as a kind of immersion journalist for the human soul. The book digs deeply into issues of life and death, hope and despair, promise and pain. And as you read Ecclesiastes, you discover the space and freedom for you to face your own skepticism, and perhaps even your cynicism. And it might even suggest to you that the only way to find ultimate meaning and purpose in God is to stretch yourself to the limits of your own humanity.

DAY 173　　　　　*Proverbs 27:1–29:27*

"As iron sharpens iron, / so one person sharpens a friend (27:17). We all need people who make us better and stronger in the faith simply by our being around them. Who are those people for you?

DAY 174　　　　　*Proverbs 30:1-33*

Proverbs 30:7-9 names two important things that we should pray for every day: 1) that we may live and speak truth, and 2) that we may have all we need, nothing more or less. Truth and contentment are pillars of wise living. How is that true for you?

DAY 175

Proverbs 31:1-31

Proverbs concludes with chapter 31 and the image of a wise, faithful woman as a metaphor for the life of wisdom. The final chapter of Proverbs describes her qualities: she is industrious, influential, strong, who does good, cares for the needy, and empowers others. What will you do to nurture these qualities for your own wise life?

DAY 176

Ecclesiastes 1:1–2:26

Ecclesiastes is a favorite biblical book for many people, as it serves as a counterweight to the altruism of Psalms and Proverbs. Ecclesiastes names reality as a place where things don't always work out for the best, where what we believe is fair or just doesn't always happen. That's often the best starting point for turning away from self and toward God. It's not about us. How is that true for you?

DAY 177 *Ecclesiastes 3:1–5:20*

Ecclesiastes 3–5 reminds us that we cannot control time, cannot ignore the evils of the world, and cannot make it on our own. But we can make the most of our time, choose joy, and control our speech and actions.

DAY 178 *Ecclesiastes 6:1–8:17*

Ecclesiastes 7:1-14 reads like the beatitudes, in that it both names and normalizes the shadow side of life. Life isn't always easy, but we should not give up. The best we can do is face each day for what it is, and remember that it is good to be alive. What hope does that encouragement bring you?

DAY 179

Ecclesiastes 9:1–12:14

We consume so much time concerned about what may or may not happen. Suffering also can happen whether we deserve it or not. Ecclesiastes 9–12 reminds us that the best and only thing we can do is live fully in the moment. How will you live more fully in the moment today?

NOTES & REFLECTIONS

Song of Solomon 1:1–Isaiah 23:18

This week's readings begin with the Song of Solomon, a beautiful poem capturing the passion of human love. The song reminds us that intimate love is both a gift from God and one of the soul's great desires, and that finding a person to share such love is one of life's greatest joys.

After that, we enter the final stage of our journey through the Old Testament, the prophetic books, beginning with Isaiah. Biblical scholars often divide the prophetic books into two sections, corresponding with the way they appear in the Jewish Tanakh: the Major Prophets, including Isaiah, Jeremiah, and Ezekiel, and the Minor Prophets, Joel through Malachi, of which there are twelve. (The distinction "major" vs. "minor" refers to the length of the prophetic books, not their importance.) Our Protestant Bibles include Lamentations after Jeremiah, because tradition associates it with Jeremiah, and Daniel after Ezekiel. In Jewish Bibles, however, Daniel is included in a separate section called the Writings, not among the prophetic books.

For many of us, this section of the Bible from Isaiah to Malachi goes widely unread and is largely unfamiliar. This is unfortunate, as its messages are as powerful and poetic as they come in the Bible. And while we may get discouraged or derailed by the strange names, places, and references in the prophets, their message is timely and relevant, and they come to us at just the right time.

The prophets give us a message we need to hear about the relationship between the kingdoms of this earth and the kingdom of God. God called the prophets as messengers to speak directly into the political realities of their day. They were the checks and balances against human institutions of power and against the systems of oppression and injustice that often came as a result. Just take a look at how the Book of Isaiah opens. The first five chapters of Isaiah run the gamut of accusations against every major empire: Assyria, Babylon, Moab, Damascus, Egypt, Edom, Arabia. Every nation throughout history has been ravaged by sinfulness and disobedience, and caused harm to its people. And the prophets like Isaiah spoke against them, bringing God's word of judgment and a call to a better way.

Isaiah is one of the most well-known and appreciated prophetic books. We read its texts during the season of Advent as we look to the birth of Jesus, and it is one of the most frequently quoted books in the New Testament, suggesting the clear connection between Isaiah's prophecies and the early church's understanding of who Jesus was and what his life, death, and resurrection meant. The book identifies itself as the work of Isaiah, son of Amoz, during the reigns of Uzziah, Jotham, Ahaz, and Hezekiah in Judah in the late 700s BC (1:1). But the book's apparent historical setting spans at least two centuries, with chapters 40–66 addressing the people of Judah after the Babylonian conquest of 587 BC. This suggests that Isaiah is actually the work of three different writers, a testament to the influence of the eighth-century prophet Isaiah and his message, which later authors sought to carry forward.

DAY 180   *Song of Solomon 1:1–4:16*

The Song of Solomon is love poetry, capturing the passion of human love. But it is also filled with metaphors and images of the natural world. It's a reminder that love encompasses all of creation, and care for the planet is an act of love and devotion. How does this change your perspective on caring for the environment?

DAY 181   *Song of Solomon 5:1–8:14*

The Bible names and normalizes many emotions: sadness, happiness, fear, anger, joy. But only the Song of Solomon names passionate, intimate love. It's one of the soul's great desires, and finding a person to share it with is one of life's greatest gifts. Who might that person be for you? For whom are you that person?

DAY 182   *Isaiah 1:1–4:6*

Isaiah may have been written nearly 2,800 years ago, but its indictments against the world and exhortations to righteousness then are just as applicable now: do right, seek justice, defend the oppressed, care for the orphan and widow, and turn weapons of war into seeds of peace. How will you contribute to those efforts?

DAY 183   *Isaiah 5:1–7:25*

The first five chapters of Isaiah paint a bleak picture of the world with its violence, injustice, evil. Isaiah 6 is what the world can be when filled with God's love: glorious, transformative, celebratory. All God needs is for us to say, as Isaiah did: "I'm here; send me" (v. 8).

DAY 184 *Isaiah 8:1–11:16*

Isaiah 8–11 contains many texts promising peace—texts that we are used to encountering in the season of Advent. But it also has hard images of crisis and pain. It's what the Israelites needed to change their views. It's nicer to be motivated by love, but sometimes crisis and pain are what push us to grow. When have you ever been positively motivated by crisis?

DAY 185 *Isaiah 12:1–16:14*

God pulls down the proud and the oppressor. But God will also pull down the oppressed if they cross the fine line to become the oppressor. It includes anyone who says "I will climb up to heaven; / above God's stars, I will raise my throne" (14:13). In what ways are you either the oppressed or the oppressor?

DAY 186 *Isaiah 17:1–23:18*

Isaiah reminds us that no nation is perfect. But Isaiah 19:18-24 envisions pockets of faithfulness seeking God's best, shining as a witness to the world. May the church be that "city of the sun" (19:18), and may we each play a part in creating it.

NOTES & REFLECTIONS

Isaiah 24:1–52:12

The Book of Isaiah is actually the work of at least two, likely three different prophets writing at different times. Isaiah 1–39 is called First Isaiah, and most of the messages there come from the eighth century BC, when the Assyrian Empire threatened Israel and Judah. We read the narrative of his calling as a prophet in Isaiah 6. Isaiah 40–55 is called Second Isaiah and comes from a writer during the time of the Babylonian Exile, as the people of Judah hoped for return to Jerusalem. Isaiah 56–66 is called Third Isaiah and may be from a later writer, or perhaps the author of Second Isaiah writing at a later time. The common thread through all these writings is a thematic, theological emphasis on righteousness, the centrality of Jerusalem, and God's holiness and steadfast presence among the people.

This week's readings conclude the first major section of Isaiah, chapters 1–39, and begin the second major portion of the book, Second Isaiah (Isaiah 40–55). Most of the prophecies in Isaiah 1–39 relate to the eighth century BC in Judah, especially the reigns of King Ahaz and King Hezekiah (see Isaiah 1:1). Isaiah 36–39 contains a set of narratives related to the reign of Hezekiah, which closely parallels and in many cases is identical with 2 Kings 18–20. These chapters mark a transition between Isaiah's prophecies during Hezekiah's reign with the ones found in Isaiah 40–66, which spoke to the people in the context of the Babylonian Exile. Isaiah 39 prefigures the Exile as messengers from Babylon visit Hezekiah and Isaiah predicts that Hezekiah's house will be carried off to Babylon.

The tone shifts beginning with Isaiah 40, which begins with the words "Comfort, comfort my people!" Second Isaiah largely brings words of comfort and reassurance, meant to give hope to those in exile, that God cares for them and continues to act for their good. Second Isaiah contains a number of important themes, including the notion of return from captivity as a second Exodus experience and the idea that the God of Israel is the only God, with all rulers and powers of the world subordinate to God's will. Idolatry is ridiculed, and even the great Persian king Cyrus is described as God's chosen instrument to bring the people of Judah back from the Exile.

Isaiah 40–55 also contains four oracles known as the Servant Songs, found in Isaiah 42:1-4; Isaiah 49:1-6; Isaiah 50:4-7; and Isaiah 52:13–53:12. These poems describe God's servant, whose identity is unknown. Some have suggested that the servant is a prophet, perhaps the writer of Second Isaiah, while others have suggested it's a future messianic figure and others a personified Israel. Christians have often identified the servant with Jesus, especially in light of the fourth servant song, which depicts the servant suffering and being "pierced because of our rebellions" (53:5).

DAY 187 *Isaiah 24:1–27:13*

Isaiah describes a world in disarray, an earth that literally quakes with turmoil (24:19). But he also depicts hope: he faithfully, calmly tends and guards his vineyard (chapter 27), believing that the fruit it bears will make a difference. May it be so for us. What are steady, personal ways that you contribute to hope in the world?

DAY 188 *Isaiah 28:1–31:9*

Isaiah 28–31 reminds us that self-help doesn't save. Forgive us, Lord, for turning to ourselves, our strength, our nationalism, our economic and military might, or anything else we have created, to give us the peace and security that you alone can provide.

DAY 189   *Isaiah 32:1–35:10*

Isaiah 32–35 reminds us that when all seems lost, it never is. God is in exile with us, rising to the challenge (33:10), strengthening us (35:3), and creating a way of justice and peace where there seems to be no way (35:5-10).

DAY 190   *Isaiah 36:1–39:8*

In Isaiah 36–39 we read the story of the good king Hezekiah for the third time in the Bible. His story again reminds us that when we are faithful to God during times of relative calm, we will be more prepared to be faithful in times of trouble.

DAY 191   *Isaiah 40:1–44:28*

If you're feeling down, fearful, or broken, read Isaiah 40–44. It not only contains some of the most often quoted words of encouragement in the Bible, it repeats this comforting refrain: "Don't fear."

DAY 192   *Isaiah 45:1–48:22*

Sin in our lives makes pleasing ourselves a higher priority than pleasing God. It gives us a false sense of security (47:10) and offers no true, lasting sense of peace (48:22). The better way is to open our eyes and ears to life as God intends it (48:6-7).

DAY 193

Isaiah 49:1–52:12

The faithful life isn't always easy. Just ask Isaiah. But God encourages you just like Isaiah. You are chosen (49:2). You are gifted (50:4). Others have gone before you (51:1-2). God comforts you (51:12) and helps you shake the dust and rise up (52:2).

NOTES & REFLECTIONS

Isaiah 52:13–Jeremiah 16:21

This week's readings conclude the Book of Isaiah and begin Jeremiah. Our first section of Isaiah is the fourth Servant Song (Isaiah 52:13–53:12), found in Second Isaiah. The fourth Servant Song describes a suffering servant, a figure the early Christians readily identified with Jesus and his death on the cross.

Jeremiah prophesied during the last days of Judah, during the years leading up to and following the destruction of Jerusalem and the exile to Babylon. These were disorienting times characterized by war, famine, death, destruction, and surely also fear, anger, and the question of God's role in such suffering. Jeremiah often described the Babylonian attack on Judah as God's punishment for breaking the covenant, but much of his words also simply gives voice to the destruction and pain that the nation experienced. And Jeremiah also offers hope for those who survive, calling them to continue in faithfulness to God and promising restoration for God's people.

Throughout the book we also see the prophet himself suffering, enduring the hostility of Jerusalem's king, rival prophets, and the people. Jeremiah's words of disaster were understandably unpopular, and many rejected him as a result. We see the prophet sparring with other prophets who predicted salvation from Babylon, at times in direct confrontation. We also see Jeremiah using symbolic actions to grab the people's attention and communicate his message. In one well-known act, Jeremiah smashes a clay jar and declares that God will smash the people of Judah in the same way (chap. 19). In another, Jeremiah purchases a field as a sign that God will bring restoration (chap. 32). Though the field and its surrounding land were then under Babylonian control, God tells Jeremiah that the people will return from captivity to possess the land once again.

Jeremiah faced the unenviable task of bringing God's messages to the people of Judah during their most painful and trying, yet also transformative period. God used Jeremiah to help the people make sense of the disaster they faced, while also calling them to respond to it first with repentance and then with hope. Jeremiah's words stand as a reminder of this critical time in the story of God's people. But perhaps even more than that, Jeremiah's steadfast obedience and perseverance showed the people of his day a compelling example of faithfulness to God when they needed it most. May his life and his message be an example for us today as well.

DAY 194
Isaiah 52:13–55:13

Isaiah 55 is full of reminders that I need God even when things are well, for that's when I put myself ahead of God and think I know it all. Listening and looking for God "does not return . . . empty" (v. 11) and leads to a life bursting with joy.

DAY 195
Isaiah 56:1–59:21

The next time you're tempted to make worship about you, read Isaiah 58. It's not about entertaining you, not about whether it "does it for you." It's not a destination; it's a hub. True worship inspires you to give of yourself to God and others.

DAY 196 *Isaiah 60:1–66:24*

Isaiah 61:1-2 is what Jesus read for his first-ever sermon. It's about good news for the down and out. Theologians remind us that, when Jesus read these verses in the synagogue, he stopped reading halfway through verse 2. Jesus chose not to say "a day of vindication for our God" (61:2; see Luke 4:16-21). Jesus was about liberation, not retribution, and we should be, too.

DAY 197 *Jeremiah 1:1–4:31*

The two worst things God can say about a person is that they are faithless or disloyal (3:11). The hardest thing God can ask a person to do is challenge both, as God called Jeremiah to do. As difficult as it must have been for Jeremiah to deliver that message, it's still better to be Jeremiah than to be Jeremiah's audience. Don't be faithless or disloyal.

DAY 198 *Jeremiah 5:1–8:17*

Jeremiah is addressing a stubborn and wayward people who are lost and scared, who are longing for a better day. His reminder was this: Do what you know you are supposed to do. Stick to the "ancient paths" and you will find your way (6:16). That's good advice for everyone.

DAY 199 *Jeremiah 8:18–12:17*

Jeremiah mourns because the people he loves are hurting themselves and there's nothing he can do to help. He's comforted by the idea that God is greater than anything he can conceive (9:23–10:16). God's holiness is greater than our helplessness.

DAY 200

Jeremiah 13:1–16:21

Jeremiah makes it very clear: bad actions have bad consequences. Sin will always be found out. We might get hung up on the idea that God punishes the Israelites with trouble, but Jeremiah reminds us that our free will gives us power to avoid bad choices.

NOTES & REFLECTIONS

Jeremiah 17:1–49:39

By the time we get to Jeremiah 30, more than halfway through its fifty-two chapters, we would begin to wonder how the people of Judah could continue to hold on to their faith. Every bit of evidence that they used to rely on to believe in God would be gone. From the glory days under King David, God's people had always relied on three pieces of evidence to prove that God was with them. Whenever they went through hardship, they need only look at three physical, external realities to remind them that God was there: the Temple, the land, and the royal line.

The Temple was a reminder of God's presence. As long as it was standing, they could believe God was there. The land was a reminder of God's provision. As long as they were living in that Promised Land given to their ancestors, they could believe God could meet their needs. And as long as a descendant of David was sitting on that throne, they could believe in God's power, and they could not be defeated.

Well, by the time we get to Jeremiah 30, we hear a prophet who would warn them, time and again, that all three of those external proofs of God's presence, provision, and power were soon going to be obliterated. That was Jeremiah's job, prophesying on the eve of the Babylonian Exile. His commission from God was to warn of disaster. He warned the people and rulers of Judah that the exile to Babylon was coming. The Temple would be destroyed, the royal line dethroned, and the people removed from their land and shipped to foreign soil.

The experience would be one of dramatic, irreversible disorientation. Predictably, the people of Judah were angered by this message from Jeremiah. Every time he would point out these disorienting times to come, the people would do something bad to him. They beat him and put him in stocks, they burned his scrolls, put a death sentence on his head, they threw him into a cistern. Few prophets were popular. But none were more unpopular than Jeremiah.

Still, through it all, Jeremiah was unwavering. And by the time we get to Jeremiah 30 and 31, we hear a word that moves from disorientation to reorientation. Jeremiah's message was that, although the external evidence that they used to rely on for courage and comfort and to hold on to God is gone, there is a new kind of evidence that will never, ever fade. And it's been with you the whole time.

> *The time is coming, declares the LORD, when I will make a new covenant with the people of Israel and Judah. It won't be like the covenant I made with their ancestors.... They broke that covenant with me.... No, this is the covenant that I will make with the people of Israel after that time, declares the LORD. I will put my Instructions within them and engrave them on their hearts. I will be their God, and they will be my people. (31:31-33)*

From now on, Jeremiah said, the evidence of God's presence, power, and provision has been placed within you. Internal, not external. And this proof will never be subject to circumstance, and it will never fade. This covenant—this relationship you have with God—will not be written on stone like the covenants of old, which fracture and crumble with the times. This covenant is written in the indelible grace of God, etched in your very heart.

DAY 201 *Jeremiah 17:1–20:18*

The truth often hurts, not just for the one hearing it, but for the one speaking it. Jeremiah had a plot made against him and was a laughingstock. Yet he still felt a "fire in his bones" to speak the truth (20:9). May we have the same boldness.

DAY 202 *Jeremiah 21:1–24:10*

Jeremiah is clear about God's problem with the people: they did nothing about injustice. They did not treat the immigrants with dignity or honor life or care for children or those without social status. Much of this indictment can apply today. What do you think can we do about it?

DAY 203   *Jeremiah 25:1–29:32*

Today's Jeremiah reading offers God's comfort and judgment. We tend to hear only the first and not the second, but we need both. The first brings us up when we are down; the second brings us back down when we see ourselves too highly.

DAY 204   *Jeremiah 30:1–33:26*

Change is hard, especially when it involves loss and grief. But God promises through Jeremiah that "the people who survived the sword / found grace in the wilderness" (31:2). And God turns "mourning into laughter / and their sadness into joy (31:13).

DAY 205   *Jeremiah 34:1–38:28*

When someone reveals to us the truth of our sins, we tend to ignore the message and denounce the messenger, like the king did in Jeremiah 36. Instead, we must confess our sins and acknowledge the consequences. Fighting only makes it worse (38:17-23).

DAY 206   *Jeremiah 39:1–45:5*

God gave a clear word to the remnant in Judea: Stay. Don't look for greener grass elsewhere. Bloom where you are planted (42:10). They should have listened, but they didn't. Sometimes the best (and hardest) thing to do is sit, watch, and wait for God.

DAY 207

Jeremiah 46:1–49:39

In Jeremiah 46–49, the prophet casts God's judgment against nine earthly empires over five chapters. No worldly power is stronger than God. It proves that we can't trust earthly systems to provide a sense of security, hope, and prosperity that only God provides.

NOTES & REFLECTIONS

Jeremiah 50:1–Ezekiel 21:32

The prophet Ezekiel spoke to the people of Judah who were in Babylon after Jerusalem was destroyed. Ezekiel was a priest, from a priestly family, and his occupation was to serve in the Temple and minister to the people. Later, God called him to be a prophet, and he brought God's words to the people in exile.

Ezekiel's identity as a priest isn't the only thing that makes him unique. The visions he received and communicated to the people were full of fantastic imagery, often more akin to what we find in the Book of Revelation than the oracles of Isaiah or Jeremiah. Of all the weird and bizarre parts of the Bible, few are stranger or more mind-altering than the Book of Ezekiel. Not only does the prophet receive and describe a series of strange, mind-altering visions, he communicates with his audience by means of dramatic, shocking symbolic acts.

The first five chapters of Ezekiel are a whirlwind of imaginative visions. He eats a sacred scroll in order to internalize God's message. He creates a play model of Jerusalem and destroys it like a kindergartner pretending to be a dinosaur. He lies on his side for a year, then the other side for forty days. He makes a weird bread out of seeds and scraps and eats it (in fact, you can find Ezekiel bread at your local grocer). And he shaves his head and burns the hair, an act of judgment based on the idea that if you have long, flowing hair, it's a sign of strength and prosperity.

But the very first image in Ezekiel is one of God. In the first chapter, we hear the story of how God called Ezekiel, who was already in Babylonian Exile at the time. It begins by describing strange beasts, with faces of humans and bodies of animals, each of them with two wings and four feet. And next to each of them were wheels. Wheels within wheels, wheels connected to other wheels, all of them pointing to various compass directions, moving in whatever directions they wish to go.

This was an image of God unlike anything the Israelites had seen in Israel. This was not an immobile God: a God seated on a fixed throne, on the Temple mountain. This was not an image of a God who filled the brick and mortar of a glorious Temple and stayed there. Those images of a God who was stationary and immovable were gone. Instead, this was a wheel. This was the image of a God of movement and adaptability, who was free and able to go in whatever direction God pleased.

In other words, this was the God who could go with them into captivity. They thought that their misery and their heartbreak was proof that God had left them or that they had left God behind. Quite the contrary, the first thing we hear from Ezekiel is that God was mobile enough to move with them into captivity. In this way Ezekiel brought a word of comfort and hope to the people in exile.

DAY 208   *Jeremiah 50:1–52:34*

Jeremiah closes with his strongest indictment yet, against the mighty Babylonians. God's most forceful judgments are against the proud and the powerful, who do not use their resources for God's purposes of love and justice.

DAY 209   *Lamentations 1:1–2:22*

Lamentations reminds us to be true to our sorrow and grief and be willing to name the hurt and pain we are feeling in our lives and in the world. For what things do we weep, with our eyes flowing with tears, with no comfort or courage to be found?

DAY 210 *Lamentations 3:1–5:22*

Lamentations 3–5 speaks for any who feel like our world has fallen apart and we feel helpless. It also gives us the assurance that God is not mad at us (3:33) and God is with us until the very end (3:22). Mostly, it gives us permission to feel what we feel.

DAY 211 *Ezekiel 1:1–5:17*

The Israelites were not hearing God, so God called Ezekiel to be a unique kind of messenger: a performance artist, whose memorable actions would speak as loud as his words. In what ways will your actions convey the truths of God's love to others?

DAY 212 *Ezekiel 6:1–11:25*

Ezekiel 6–11 shows how it feels like to be in crisis, facing disaster. We feel helpless against pain and harm. We feel like God is against us or absent. We feel like our values have been challenged. But at the end, God can change our hearts.

DAY 213 *Ezekiel 12:1–16:63*

Ezekiel 12–16 reminds us that God takes sin seriously. God relentlessly works to remove our sin and make us more like Jesus every day, so that God's love flows freely in and through us. It's our job to work with God to make that happen.

DAY 214

Ezekiel 17:1–21:32

Ezekiel 18 reminds us that much of the violence and death in the world stems from injustice and the unwillingness of people to treat one another with equity and dignity. God has no pleasure in any death and wants us to have a new heart and spirit.

NOTES & REFLECTIONS

Ezekiel 22:1–Daniel 6:28

The Book of Daniel is like a literary rest stop in our journey through the prophets. For the last several weeks, we have been reading through long, dusty stretches of Isaiah, Jeremiah, and Ezekiel. One lengthy pronouncement and oracle after another, for miles on end. And for me, there have been several points along the way when I've thought, "I can't wait to get back to some good old-fashioned storytelling."

Well, here we are. With Daniel we not only get back to some stories, but these are some of the most famous stories in the entire Old Testament. Daniel and his special diet. His successful interpretation of Nebuchadnezzar's dream. His three friends in the fiery furnace. Daniel himself in the lions' den ("pit of lions," CEB).

Even though the Book of Daniel is included in the section of the prophets, Daniel is not a prophet in the formal sense. He is not called by God to be a messenger; he doesn't speak directly to the exiles in Babylon. In fact, the biblical evidence suggests that the Book of Daniel dates much later than the Exile, to the second century BC. Instead of a single message spoken to an audience, what we find in the first six chapters of Daniel are narratives, stories of Daniel and his friends that stand as an example of how to live faithfully in exile. Daniel's very life is the spoken word about how to stay faithful and true to God, rather than bend to the ways of the world and the culture.

Daniel's experiences illustrate the chief principles of life in exile: remain faithful to God above all else, stay true to your faith, and even the rulers of other nations will recognize God's spirit working in and through you. Time and again, in the court of Nebuchadnezzar, then Belshazzar, then Darius, Daniel's faithfulness to God sets him apart, makes him successful, and leads to the ruler recognizing the greatness and power of Israel's God, the one true God.

As we hear these stories, we come to realize that they all have one thing in common. They are all stories about integrity. About how to maintain your principles and your values when everything around you is working against you. Through these stories in the first six chapters, we find that integrity was Daniel's superpower. He didn't have the ability to part the Red Sea like Moses did. He couldn't call down fire like Elijah did. He didn't conquer foreign armies like David did. All he had was the power to stay true to his values and not to compromise his convictions.

Say what you will about the miraculous elements of these stories. The greatest power demonstrated in Daniel chapters 1–6 is not just a God who protected people from being burned or devoured. It was God who helped Daniel and his friends say no to temptation and yes to their integrity.

DAY 215   *Ezekiel 22:1–26:21*

As much as we might believe in an all-powerful God, Ezekiel reminds us that there is one important thing that God cannot do: God cannot force us to be faithful. We have the power to choose to obey God or not. When we don't, we live with the consequences.

DAY 216   *Ezekiel 27:1–32:32*

Ezekiel 27–32 contains judgments over two of the greatest economic empires in the ancient Near East: Tyre and Egypt. Their downfall is a reminder that economic and military might do not provide the kind of security that only obedience to God can provide.

DAY 217 *Ezekiel 33:1–37:28*

Ezekiel 36–37 has three images of hope: 1) God will replace our hearts of stone with hearts of flesh, 2) God will breathe new life into our dry bones, and 3) God will bring unity out of division. This is good news for a people and a world that feel like they are in exile. Which image of hope speaks the most to you today?

DAY 218 *Ezekiel 38:1–42:20*

Ezekiel 40–48 is a highly detailed vision of the restored Temple and its worship. It imagines the fulfillment of God's promise in the future that gives courage in the present. We should live today with the assurance that what God promises, God will fulfill.

DAY 219

Ezekiel 43:1–48:35

Up until now, Ezekiel was envisioning a brighter future for the Israelites. But 43:10-11 is an important pivot: God says, "Now make it happen." Often, the best word of hope we have is this: God is calling you to act. You are not as helpless as you think. So get busy.

DAY 220

Daniel 1:1–3:30

Daniel 1–3 is a call to nonviolent resistance against those in power whose paranoia and narcissism incite fear and violence. Daniel and his friends choose holiness instead, and they are not just protected—God uses them to transform the world.

DAY 221

Daniel 4:1–6:28

Sometimes faithfulness looks like staring down fear and refusing to compromise God's values, even if walking in integrity means being thrown into the lions' den. If that's you today, may God "shut the lions' mouths" around you (6:22).

NOTES & REFLECTIONS

Daniel 7:1–Amos 9:15

The Book of Daniel has two major sections. Daniel 1–6 is a collection of narratives about Daniel and his friends in the courts of Babylonian and Persian kings, well-known stories that highlight the importance of remaining faithful to God. Daniel 7–12 is a series of apocalyptic visions that Daniel receives, which depict heavenly conflict, fantastical creatures, symbolic imagery, angelic messengers, and ultimately the triumph of God and God's people over the kingdoms of the world. Much of the imagery in Daniel 7–12 recurs in the New Testament, including in the Book of Revelation. Daniel 7:13 describes "one like a human being" or "one like a son of man," which later Jewish interpreters came to regard as a messianic figure. Jesus's self-description as the Human One or the Son of Man likely alludes to Daniel 7:13.

This week's readings also include the books of Hosea, Joel, and Amos. It's difficult to link Joel with a specific time period, as the book provides few concrete historical references. It does mention a devastating locust plague, which Joel laments and sees as evidence of God's judgment, a signal that the "day of the Lord" has arrived.

Hosea and Amos were two eighth-century prophets in the Northern Kingdom of Israel. Hosea portrays God's relationship with Israel as a marriage, in which God is the husband and Israel the wife. Israel's worship of other gods is likened to marital unfaithfulness, which both grieves and angers God. The book opens with God commanding Hosea to marry a woman named Gomer who will be unfaithful and sleep with other men. This may be understood as a symbolic action, meant to convey God's message through the prophet in a deeper way than words alone could communicate. What's clear throughout Hosea is the passionate emotional connection God feels to Israel, which Hosea himself feels through his marriage to Gomer. The broken covenant grieves and hurts God, and God desires nothing more than to see the relationship restored.

Amos speaks of coming judgment against Israel for a lack of justice and righteousness. He calls out the Northern Kingdom for oppressing its people and for worshipping idols. Amos describes himself as a shepherd whom God called to bring a word to the people. He may have been a resident of Judah, the Southern Kingdom, whom God sent to Israel. Amos pronounced God's judgment on several surrounding nations, including Judah (1:1–2:5) before turning his attention to Israel to foretell its destruction beginning at 2:6. Amos's followers likely understood his words to have been fulfilled when the Assyrians destroyed the Northern Kingdom of Israel in 722 BC.

DAY 222

Daniel 7:1–12:13

Daniel ends with an apocalyptic vision in the style of Revelation. It is written to sound like predictions of the future, but are mostly meant to encourage us in the present: no matter what happens, we must be faithful, and God will triumph. How might these be good words for today?

DAY 223

Hosea 1:1–5:15

Hosea shows us the challenge of having to love a person or persons who are causing harm to themselves and others. But there is encouragement: Hosea 3 offers transformation that comes from tough love, which is what God sometimes has to have with us. What might tough love look like to you?

DAY 224 *Hosea 6:1–10:15*

Hosea reminds us that religious actions alone aren't enough, nor are pious hearts. We need both. We need hearts that are true and actions that are faithful to live life as God intends it.

DAY 225 *Hosea 11:1–14:9*

Hosea ends on a word of promise and hope. You may feel down and out, and wonder where God is, or if God even cares. But God will heal you. God is not angry at you, and God will bring beauty into your life.

DAY 226 *Joel 1:1–3:21*

Joel 2 contains two lectionary passages we hear each year: we read verses 2:12-13 on Ash Wednesday, and we read verses 2:28-29 on Pentecost Sunday. Repentance and receiving the Spirit's power are tied together. You can't do the first without the second, and the second fully comes through the first.

DAY 227 *Amos 1:1–4:13*

No nations were perfect in the time of Amos, but the toughest judgments were on the Israelites for oppressing the poor, dehumanizing the needy, and practicing sexual promiscuity. The bottom line is this: practice compassion and fidelity with one another.

DAY 228

When everything seems to be in chaos and disarray, get back to the basics. Return to what you know God wants you to do and be. Seek the Lord. Be faithful. Do justice. Making it more complicated than that may just make things worse.

NOTES & REFLECTIONS

Obadiah–Habakkuk 3:19

This week's readings continue the Minor Prophets with Obadiah, Jonah, Micah, Nahum, and Habakkuk. Obadiah is the shortest book of the Old Testament, just a single chapter and twenty-one verses long. The book pronounces judgment against Edom, a nation that neighbored Israel and Judah and that the Bible describes as descendants of Esau, Jacob's brother. Obadiah describes Edom's celebration when the Babylonians destroyed Jerusalem and deported its people, and says that Edom will be destroyed and God's people Judah lifted up.

Situated between Obadiah and Micah, Jonah has a different quality from most of the other prophetic works. Most of the book is a narrative, describing God's call to Jonah to prophesy to Nineveh and Jonah's unwillingness to deliver the message of doom. When he finally does so, and Nineveh repents, Jonah is angry with God for sparing the city. The book has been described as a parable and as a satire, a narrative reflection on the role of prophets. But it also lifts up God's compassion and willingness to forgive. It stands in contrast to Nahum, which depicts God's judgment on Nineveh.

Micah dates to the eighth century BC in Judah, around the same time as Isaiah. The book announces God's judgment on Judah, saying that "the Lord is coming out from his place" because of "the crime of Jacob / and the sins of the house of Israel" (1:3-5). The punishment that befell Israel in the form of the Assyrian Empire made its way to Judah as well. At the same time, Micah also contains words of hope.

Nahum announces God's judgment on Nineveh, the capital of the Assyrian Empire that destroyed Israel and devastated Judah. Where Jonah portrays God's compassion toward the Assyrian inhabitants of the city, Nahum describes their destruction in violent terms. Habakkuk wrestles with the question of why unrighteous people flourish, including both the people of Judah who act violently and the Babylonians whom God is sending to punish Judah.

DAY 229 *Obadiah 1-21*

Obadiah reminds us that even though Jacob and Esau had reconciled thousands of years earlier, their descendants (Israel and Edom) never fully made peace. Sins of racism and nationalism linger; they require constant repentance and reconciliation.

DAY 230 *Jonah 1:1–2:10*

Jonah's three days in the fish were a blessing, not a punishment. In three days, he went through three critical stages of spiritual transformation: 1) disorientation or distress; 2) prayer, thanksgiving, surrender; and 3) release to make a difference. What might those steps look like in your life?

DAY 231 *Jonah 3:1–4:11*

Jonah was mad that God forgave the enemy. He had come full circle: resistance to God's call at the start, then repulsion at God's grace at the end. God's circle of love is wider than our cycle of sin. It forgives our enemies around us, and it transforms the enemy within us.

DAY 232 *Micah 1:1–4:13*

In Micah 2–3, God is like a prosecuting attorney, and God's people are the defendants, accused of injustice, inequality, war-mongering, and religious hypocrisy. But in Micah 4, God turns into a compassionate judge who offers redemption, not punishment. What difference should that make in you?

DAY 233
Micah 5:1–7:20

In Micah 6:8 we read of the three things God requires of us: Do justice. Love kindness. Walk humbly with God. These are not multiple choice. They are not mix-and-match. Fully living out each one is impossible without the other two.

DAY 234
Nahum 1:1–3:19

In the Book of Jonah, Nineveh is envisioned as having repented and chosen to follow God. The Book of Nahum paints a different picture, with the prophet pronouncing judgment and doom on Nineveh and Assyria. Repentance is not a one-time task. It is a daily choice to live as God intends and not to sin.

DAY 235 *Habakkuk 1:1–3:19*

Amid all the heartbreak Habakkuk is experiencing, God tells him to stand tall, keep watch, and wait for hope, because the vision awaits the time. The book concludes with his response: Despite all that is going wrong, "I will rejoice" (3:18). How will you hope and rejoice today?

NOTES & REFLECTIONS

Zephaniah 1:1–Malachi 4:6

This week concludes our time in the Old Testament with the final four of the Minor Prophets: Zephaniah, Haggai, Zechariah, and Malachi.

Zephaniah's opening lines attribute it to Zephaniah, son of Cushi, during the days of King Josiah of Judah, who instituted a series of religious reforms to bring the nation back into observation of God's covenant. Zephaniah's prophecies may have been linked with Josiah's reforms. The prophet speaks of the coming "day of the LORD" on which God will bring disaster on the kingdom of Judah and Jerusalem, as well as on foreign nations including Assyria. Despite the punishment decreed for Jerusalem, Zephaniah ends on a word of hope that Daughter Jerusalem will be restored.

Haggai and Zechariah both date to the Persian period, sometime around 520 BC, when the people of Jerusalem were attempting to rebuild the Temple that had been destroyed by the Babylonians in 587 BCE. Haggai exhorted the people to rebuild the Temple, bringing God's words to encourage their efforts. Zechariah 1–8 relates a series of visions that deal with the rebuilding of the Temple, while Zechariah 9–14 is a prophetic word about the return of Judah's king and the corresponding preparation that the people and priests must make before his arrival. It is Zechariah where we find the prophecy quoted on Palm Sunday that Jerusalem's king will come riding on a donkey (9:9).

Malachi also appears to date to the Persian period, though little is known about the author. The word *Malachi* means "my messenger," so it may be the name of the prophet or it may be a title indicating that the unnamed prophet is God's messenger. Unlike Haggai and Zechariah, which address the rebuilding of the Temple, Malachi focuses on the people maintaining a strong relationship with God. The prophet advocates proper observances of worship and keeping God's covenant. Malachi ends with a prophecy about the coming day of the Lord on which the "sun of righteousness will rise" (4:2) on those who fear God. God will send Elijah before that day to prepare the people. It is a fitting end to the Old Testament in Christian Bibles, as the New Testament will open with John the Baptist, identified as God's messenger Elijah who prepares the way for the coming of Christ.

DAY 236 *Zephaniah 1:1–3:20*

Zephaniah doesn't make many people's lists of favorite Bible books. It promotes faithfulness using fear and anger. Still, with everything wrong in the world today, it's comforting to think that God is as upset by it all as we are, and God refuses to sit still and let it happen.

DAY 237 *Haggai 1:1–2:23*

Haggai may be an obscure book, but it packs a timely punch: Get your priorities straight. You may seem to live a great life, but if your spiritual life isn't in order, then it's wasted energy. You are sowing much but harvesting little, eating but not being filled.

DAY 238   *Zechariah 1:1–4:14*

To anyone who feels like they are living in exile, Zechariah promises that God will return with prosperity, comfort, and forgiveness of sins. This won't happen because of human might or power, but by God's Spirit alone (4:6).

DAY 239   *Zechariah 5:1–9:17*

When Matthew and John described the arrival of Jesus in Jerusalem, they refer to Zechariah 9:9 ("humble and riding on a ass"). It's a reminder that true greatness is not measured by conquests, but by servanthood and humility.

DAY 240 *Zechariah 10:1–14:21*

Zechariah 11 reminds us that we carry two responsibilities, symbolized by the two staffs: "Delight" and "Harmony." The first represents our commitment to God, while the second represents our relationships with one another. Unfortunately, the Israelites have broken both. We should not.

DAY 241 *Malachi 1:1–2:17*

Malachi asks, "Have we not all one father? . . . Why then are we faithless to one another?" (2:10 NRSV). It is a reminder that faithfulness to God requires treating others with dignity and respect. Doing otherwise is tiring to the Lord (2:17).

DAY 242

Malachi 3:1–4:6

The Old Testament closes with the promise of the Messiah (future) and a reminder of Moses and Elijah (past). The faithful life is based on remembering what God has told you in order to claim what God has promised you. Now, on to the New Testament!

NOTES & REFLECTIONS

PART 2

THE NEW TESTAMENT

Matthew–Revelation

Matthew 1:1–12:50

In most of our Bibles, it is a simple flip of a page to get from the Old Testament to the New Testament. One page turn gets us from the last chapter of Malachi to the first chapter of Matthew.

But in historical terms, that single page turn sweeps past four hundred years of time between the testaments. Four centuries after the ministry of Malachi and the completion of the Temple until the arrival of John the Baptist and the birth of Jesus. In that single page turn of four centuries, the world changed. Ruling empires rose and fell, from the Persians to the Greeks under Alexander the Great, to the Ptolemies and Seleucids as Alexander's successors, then the Romans and their Caesars. The global culture and economy changed with the arrival of Hellenism, as Greek ideas exerted their undeniable influence and Roman roads fostered travel and commerce.

The people known as the Israelites through much of the Old Testament would now be known as the Jews in the New Testament. And they would continue to live under foreign rule, as unwilling pawns in the shifting of one empire to the next. Many struggled to maintain the purity of Jewish tradition and law, and many others changed with the times and embraced Greco-Roman culture and practices. In the midst of it all there arose a new teaching assembly called the synagogue, and a new religious group known as the Pharisees who studied and practiced the law with utmost care and devotion.

Into this world, Jesus of Nazareth was born. He proclaimed the kingdom of God and gathered twelve disciples to follow him. He taught, healed, worked wonders among the people, first in Galilee and then in Judea. He was crucified by the Romans at the urging of Jewish religious leaders. Three days later he rose from the dead, appeared to his disciples, and commissioned them to carry on his message of salvation.

The New Testament begins with four books, called Gospels, that tell the story of Jesus. Matthew, Mark, Luke, and John each present us with a different picture of the man Jesus, known as the Messiah, or Christ, and the Son of God. Each writer tells the story differently, capturing different aspects of who Jesus was and what his life, ministry, death, and resurrection meant.

In discussing the parables of Jesus, New Testament scholar John Dominic Crossan identifies a three-part movement of God's kingdom: Advent-Reversal-Action. He highlights these aspects by exploring specific parables that exemplify each one (*In Parables: The Challenge of the Historical Jesus* [Polebridge Press, 1992], 31-36). This three-word phrase, Advent-Reversal-Action, helps us identify the distinguishing message of the Gospel of Matthew.

Here's what that means. In most of these stories and teachings in Matthew, there is first an advent or arrival of Jesus, in which he breaks into the scene and illuminates what is broken about the world or the human condition. And there is a reversal, in which Jesus takes conventional wisdom, conventional religious teachings, normal ways of seeing the world, and flips them upside down. And then there is a call to action, in which what Jesus says and does demands the hearer (and the reader) to change something about themselves.

As you read the opening chapters of Matthew, watch for this three-fold movement, Advent-Reversal-Action, especially in chapters 5–7, the Sermon on the Mount.

DAY 243   *Matthew 1:1–2:23*

Welcome to the New Testament. Out of the gate, Matthew asks, What will you do with fear? Will it lead to anger and paranoia, as was the case with Herod? Or will you trust God, even when it doesn't make sense, as Joseph and the magi did? When we are afraid, God calls us to trust and go.

DAY 244   *Matthew 3:1–4:25*

In Matthew 3–4, the prophets are quoted five times, by John the Baptist, Jesus, and the writer of Matthew. The story of Jesus is rooted in a knowledge of the Scriptures. May the story of our lives be anchored in the same way, so that we are living out the truth of the Bible.

DAY 245 *Matthew 5:1-48*

The five most important words in Matthew 5 are, "But I say to you." Each time Jesus says that, he tells us that righteous behavior is not enough, unless it is motivated by a pure heart. Ask yourself: "Is my heart fully in love with God and others today?"

DAY 246 *Matthew 6:1-34*

Your spiritual maturity is gauged by what you do in private, hidden from public view. Surrender your private life to God, and you can surrender your whole life to God. A way to do that is to release your worry about material things.

DAY 247 *Matthew 7:1–8:34*

In Matthew 8, Jesus shows mastery over physical illness. But before that, in chapter 7, he shows us how to have mastery over ourselves: don't judge, seek God's best, love others, choose the hard way to follow Jesus, bear fruit, and do what he commands.

DAY 248 *Matthew 9:1–10:42*

Often when Jesus healed someone, the Pharisees criticized him. In their view, he could do no right. But he wasn't discouraged. He knew his mission wasn't to make everyone happy, but to give everyone the choice to follow him. Jesus demonstrates for us how to stay focused on what God wants us to do.

DAY 249

Matthew 11:1–12:50

Jesus goes on offense against the religious hypocrites, using the healing miracles to call out their lack of compassion, their heartless legalism, their slander, and their lack of belief. Don't be a Pharisee.

NOTES & REFLECTIONS

Matthew 13:1–25:46

As we continue in the Gospel of Matthew, we will encounter more events from Jesus's life and ministry, events with which we are likely familiar. Parables and other teachings; miracles; predictions about Jesus's suffering; the triumphal entry into Jerusalem. Matthew, Mark, and Luke all relate many of these same events. But only Matthew records the teaching in Matthew 25:31-46, about the sheep and the goats. And this teaching is a clue about Matthew's theology.

The Human One, Jesus says, will gather all the nations before him and separate them, like a shepherd dividing the sheep from the goats. They are separated based on whether or not they fed him or clothed him or gave him something to drink or visited him.

The sheep are surprised, asking, "Lord, when did we see you hungry and feed you, or thirsty and give you a drink? When did we see you as a stranger and welcome you, or naked and give you clothes to wear? When did we see you sick or in prison and visit you?" (Matthew 25:37-39).

And the king answers, "I assure you that when you have done it for one of the least of these brothers and sisters of mine, you have done it for me" (25:40).

Matthew wants to impress upon us that Jesus is with us. We don't need to wait for him to return; he is here with us, right now. Matthew calls Jesus Emmanuel, which means "God with us." The return of Jesus is not some future expectation; it is a present reality. The Gospel concludes with these final words from Jesus to the disciples: "Go and make disciples of all nations, baptizing them in the name of the Father and of the Son and of the Holy Spirit....Look, I myself will be with you every day until the end of this present age."

Only Matthew records Jesus saying that. Because Jesus is already here. And always will be. Matthew 25 shows us that we can find and serve Jesus in "the least of these." Matthew's message is this: God is with us, and it is our job to live in both expectation and responsibility. To live with an eye on the future, but hands firmly engaged in the present. To live in the hope that the kingdom of God will break into the brokenness of the world, but also to live each day seeking to do the work of the Kingdom here and now. There, we will find Jesus.

DAY 250   *Matthew 13:1-58*

There are seven parables in Matthew 13, with this common idea: God is at work in your life; it may seem small, but it's real. So you have a choice: let that work grow, or choke and hide it. Don't be like those who live their entire life and miss out.

DAY 251   *Matthew 14:1–15:39*

Matthew 14 describes what may have been the longest two days of Jesus's ministry: grief over John the Baptist's death, feeding the five thousand, walking on water, and arguing with the Pharisees, all in forty-eight hours. But here's the model for us: twice in that period, he withdrew to pray.

DAY 252 *Matthew 16:1–18:35*

Matthew 16–18 is the Gospel's pivot. Peter confesses Jesus to be the Messiah, then the Transfiguration happens, then Jesus teaches reconciliation. It's a reminder that calling Jesus "Lord" means full surrender to God and full restoration with others.

DAY 253 *Matthew 19:1–20:34*

Matthew 19–20 is full of reversals. Children are blessed, the last are first, the materialistic are burdened, early and late laborers are treated the same, and the served become the servants. God's grace contradicts the world's ways. That's good news for us. How might you live more "counterculturally"?

DAY 254   *Matthew 21:1-46*

In Matthew 21, Jesus overturned the tables because the Temple wasn't being used for its holy purpose. The same is true for our lives. If we compromise the work that God wants to do in us, we are like a fruitless fig tree, a disobedient child, or a rebellious worker.

DAY 255   *Matthew 22:1–23:39*

Matthew 22–23 is the last verbal showdown between Jesus and the Pharisees. They test him with four questions about his authority, then he pronounces six woes against them for their hypocrisy. Struggles with doubt are understandable. But hypocrisy is inexcusable.

DAY 256   *Matthew 24:1–25:46*

The parable of the sheep and the goats in Matthew 25:31-46 is a reminder that if you're waiting for Jesus to come back, stop waiting. Jesus is already here. You can see him in the faces of the hungry, the thirsty, the immigrant, the poor, and the prisoner.

NOTES & REFLECTIONS

Matthew 26:1–Mark 10:45

Long before there was Agatha Christie or Sir Arthur Conan Doyle, there was Mark the Gospel writer. Matthew may have been traditionally known as the tax collector, Luke the doctor, John the beloved. But Mark— Mark was the storyteller.

Mark is the shortest of the four Gospels, the earliest one written, and it gets right to the action. It moves briskly, from one action scene to the next, often using the word *immediately*, which Mark uses nearly forty times. More than that, Mark's Gospel is like a mystery novel, in which one person after another thinks they have Jesus figured out, only for us to discover at the end a surprising twist that we did not see coming. And it is that twist that makes all the difference—not just in our understanding of Mark, but in the way we can live right now, today.

There's something about a well-told story—especially a mystery/ suspense kind of story—that makes you see the whole story differently once you know the ending. Mark's Gospel, as it turns out, is just like that.

The action in Mark picks up right away, out of the gate. No long, drawn-out genealogy like in Matthew, no series of songs like in Luke, no poetic prologue like in John. Mark the storyteller stands before the audience and begins almost immediately with Jesus bursting onto the scene, in a region of Israel called Galilee. For the next fifteen chapters, Jesus and the disciples crisscross Galilee and then go to Jerusalem, with Jesus performing miraculous healings and uttering profound teachings. But at nearly every turn in Mark's Gospel, there is a mystery surrounding who Jesus is. Every time someone comes close to guessing who Jesus really is, Jesus shuts them down.

In the very first chapter, Jesus casts out demons from people, but when the demons recognize him as the Son of God, he immediately silences them and does not allow them to speak. When he heals a leper, he orders the man not to say a word to anybody about what he has done for him. Later, when he tells the people parables, he intentionally makes it so that not everyone can understand what the parables mean. In chapter 8, when Peter declares that Jesus is the Christ, the Messiah, Jesus immediately instructs him not to tell anyone. He does the same after he is transfigured before Peter, James, and John.

It's only at the end, when Jesus is crucified and then raised from the dead, that it becomes clear who Jesus is and what that means. Mark is a master storyteller, and once we get to the end, the story of Jesus's resurrection is like an invitation to go back and read the Gospel again, this time with the Resurrection in mind. As you are reading these stories of Mark over the next several days, ask this question of the text: What does this passage tell me about the power of the Resurrection?

And then take it one step further. Because Mark is asking us to look at the story of our lives with the very same filter: How is God doing the work of resurrection in your life? How is God doing the work of resurrection in the world?

DAY 257 *Matthew 26:1-75*

Matthew 26 calls us to choose: Will our faith in Christ be marked more by the expensive perfume used by the woman at Bethany to anoint him, or by the thirty pieces of silver used by Judas to betray him? Choose sacrifice, not betrayal.

DAY 258 *Matthew 27:1–28:20*

Matthew ends with two competing stories: the cover-up and the commission. There's the story that the disciples stole Jesus's body, and there's the command by Jesus to go into the world and make disciples. We are called to disprove the former by being the proof of the latter.

DAY 259   *Mark 1:1–3:35*

It's interesting that in Mark and Luke, the first miracle Jesus performs is healing the man with the "unclean spirit," which is how the Bible describes mental illness. From the outset, Jesus cared for people with mental illness. We should too.

DAY 260   *Mark 4:1–5:43*

Until now, Jesus healed many people, but insisted they keep it a secret. Then in Mark 5, he cast a man's demons into swine and healed him, and told him to tell everyone about his healing. Again, Mark emphasizes Jesus's heart for the mentally hurting.

DAY 261

Mark 6:1-56

Mark 6 captures the whole range of human anxieties: rejection, grief, fatigue and hunger, panic and overwork, and ill health. But above it all, Jesus says, "Be encouraged! It's me. Don't be afraid" (v. 50). May his words bring encouragement to you.

DAY 262

Mark 7:1–8:38

The pivot point in Mark 8 is verses 11-13; the other stories before and after run parallel to each other. Here Jesus tells the Pharisees there will be no heavenly sign to prove his authority. If you're looking for proof, note the transformed lives around you.

DAY 263

Mark 9:1–10:45

Mark 9–10 has three reminders that true greatness is found through servanthood and humility: Whoever wants to be first will be last. Those with a childlike faith will enter the Kingdom. And Jesus did not come to be served, but to serve.

NOTES & REFLECTIONS

Mark 10:46–Luke 4:13

This week you will conclude the Gospel of Mark and begin the Gospel of Luke. You will begin to notice, if you haven't already, that Matthew, Mark, and Luke contain many of the same stories and teachings from Jesus. Each of these Gospels has its unique features: only Matthew contains the story of the magi and the Holy Family's flight to Egypt, while only Luke has the story of the angels appearing to shepherds the night Jesus was born. Luke and Matthew record different genealogies of Jesus, and all three describe Jesus's baptism and temptation in the wilderness in slightly different ways.

Despite these differences, however, each of the three Gospels gives us the same basic picture we get of the major events of Jesus's ministry, and of the things he taught. For this reason, Matthew, Mark, and Luke are known as the "Synoptic Gospels." (The word *synoptic* means "seeing together.") Most New Testament scholars attribute this similarity to shared sources about Jesus's life, though the exact nature of these sources is debated. The most prominent idea is that the Gospel of Mark was written first, and that both Luke and Matthew drew upon Mark as a source. Luke and Matthew also drew on a separate source, now lost, which accounts for material found in Luke and Matthew but not in Mark.

Interestingly, the author of Luke opens by describing other accounts of Jesus's life, saying that he has "investigated everything carefully from the beginning" and has now set out to write a new, "carefully ordered account" (see 1:1-4). One purpose Luke has in writing is for his audience to have confidence in the good news about Jesus, which is reinforced by Luke's careful investigation.

The parallels among Matthew, Mark, and Luke give us an opportunity to ask what significance each author sees in Jesus's life and teaching. What do they choose to emphasize in a given story? What do they include that is unique, and why? The Gospel writers, like the writers of the Old Testament as well, are concerned not just with telling us what happened, but with communicating to us the meaning and significance of it. By paying close attention to the similarities and differences among Matthew, Mark, and Luke, we can gain a more complete understanding of Jesus's identity as God's Son and the salvation he brings through his life, ministry, death, and resurrection.

DAY 264

Mark 10:46–12:34

This is Mark's odd version of Palm Sunday. After Jesus entered Jerusalem, he left that night and returned the next day to curse the fig tree and cleanse the Temple. That's grace. We're never so low that we can't say "Hosanna!" and never so high that we don't need our sins cleansed.

DAY 265

Mark 12:35–13:37

Mark 13 contains the "little apocalypse," where Jesus forecasts the Roman persecution and the destruction of the Temple. But his biggest warning is against the Pharisees, for taking advantage of the poor. Injustice and inequality are in themselves destructive. How do we hear and heed that warning for ourselves?

DAY 266   *Mark 14:1-72*

Mark 14 is about blind spots. Jesus knew something about the disciples that they didn't acknowledge in themselves: their capacity to betray, deny, and fall away from him. Following Jesus means confessing our tendency to say, Surely not I?

DAY 267   *Mark 15:1–16:20*

The Gospel that begins with Jesus casting out demons ends with Jesus empowering the disciples to do the same. Yes, there is evil in this broken world. But God is greater, and we are called and equipped to do something about it.

DAY 268
Luke 1:1-80

Luke begins with a unifying vision of the old (Elizabeth) and the young (Mary) joining together to usher in the Kingdom. All generations are important; they each have value to offer one another. What can you learn today from people older and younger than you?

DAY 269
Luke 2:1-52

Sometimes the spiritual life is filled with bold, indelible moments of glory to God (angels, shepherds). Sometimes it is filled with quiet, centered "pondering" (Mary, v. 19 NRSV). Regardless of how today goes, find time to praise through pondering.

DAY 270

Luke 3:1–4:13

It's interesting that while Matthew puts Jesus's genealogy at the time of his birth, Luke puts it at the outset of his ministry. We have two ancestries: one that led to the start of our lives, and the one that led to the start of our faith. Both are important.

NOTES & REFLECTIONS

Luke 4:14–14:35

When I think of the Gospel of Luke, and when I think about its central message that distinguishes itself from the other three gospels, the quality that is uniquely Luke, I think of a scene from the film *Forrest Gump*.

It's the scene toward the beginning of the movie that begins with the boy Forrest getting on the school bus for the first time. If you've seen the movie, you know the scene.

Young Forrest steps up onto the bus, his mother waving goodbye in the background, and he then looks over the entire bus to find an empty seat. He begins walking down the aisle and spots a few vacant seats next to some boys. The first boy says with a growl, "This seat is taken." The second boy in another row glares at him. "It's taken," he says. Row after row, seat after seat gets the same response. Forrest can't find a seat where someone would allow him to sit next to them. But then, finally, a young girl named Jenny motions Forrest to the empty seat next to her. "You can sit here," Jenny says.

That scene captures a central message of the Gospel of Luke.

If Matthew is about showing us a different way to live, and if Mark is about experiencing the Resurrection every day, then the good news according to the Gospel of Luke is that God's love is inclusive, and welcomes everyone to have a seat on the bus.

As you read through Luke over the next couple of weeks, you will discover along the way many, many stories that are unique to Luke's Gospel and reinforce this point. Last week in Scripture you read about an old man named Simeon who picked up the baby Jesus and declared him as a "light for revelation to the Gentiles" (2:32). You heard John the Baptist say the phrase, "all humanity will see God's salvation" (3:6). In this week's first reading, you'll see Jesus declare his mission in his very first sermon, in his hometown, where he says that he has come "to preach good news to the poor, to proclaim release to the prisoners and recovery of sight to the blind, to liberate the oppressed" (4:18).

Luke also contains the story of the good Samaritan, in which a foreigner is the hero who helps the man on the side of the road. And it's Luke in which you will find the parable of the often-called "prodigal son," whom the father welcomes home despite his wayward living. And then, of course, Luke also wrote the Book of Acts, which is filled with examples of God's love expanding wider and wider to include more and more people.

As you are reading through the Gospel of Luke, I hope you'll pay attention to the way Jesus's salvation includes all people. I encourage you to use this as the guiding question in each story. Ask yourself, "What does this passage tell me about God's inclusive love, in which all are welcome?"

DAY 271 *Luke 4:14–5:39*

Luke 5 contains the beautiful story of the people who lower their friend through the roof to meet Jesus. Who do you know who needs to be healed by Jesus? What friends reflect Jesus for you? How might you see the "strange things" of God's grace today?

DAY 272 *Luke 6:1-49*

Just think of how much better this world would be if we all lived out Luke 6:37-42. Don't judge. Don't condemn. Forgive. Don't search for specks in other's eyes when you have a log in your own. Imagine how better our relationships, country, and world would be.

DAY 273 *Luke 7:1–8:39*

There are only two people in the Gospels who amazed Jesus by their faith. One is the Canaanite woman (Matthew 15), the other is the centurion in Luke; both were outsiders to the Jews. This calls us to expand our view of God's love to include those that others would exclude.

DAY 274 *Luke 8:40–9:62*

Only Luke records the story in 9:51-56, where the disciples want to punish a Samaritan village with fire from heaven because the villagers rejected them. But Jesus rebuked the disciples. The way of violence and revenge is never the way of Jesus.

DAY 275

Luke 10:1–11:36

The good Samaritan story is placed in the middle of teachings about rejection, perseverance, and suffering. It's a reminder that no matter how bad life gets, we can always be in service to our neighbor in need.

DAY 276

Luke 11:37–12:59

Hardly a day goes by when Luke 12:13-34 isn't helpful in some way. Don't be obsessed with possessions. Do not worry. Do not be afraid. Keep your priorities straight. We are more than lilies and sparrows. We are the "little flock" of God.

DAY 277   *Luke 13:1–14:35*

We typically interpret the mustard seed parable to suggest that we should have "faith like a mustard seed." But given the story Luke tells before this, it could also mean having "compassion like a mustard seed." Even a little goes a long way.

NOTES & REFLECTIONS

Luke 15:1–24:53

As we conclude the Gospel of Luke this week, we encounter a number of passages that are unique to Luke, with no corresponding version in Matthew and Mark.

Luke 15 contains three parables about finding the lost and the celebration someone feels when this happens. The Pharisees and legal experts took issue with Jesus eating and fellowshipping with sinners and tax collectors. In response, Jesus tells them a parable of a shepherd with a hundred sheep, losing one and leaving the others behind to look for it. Luke follows that with a second parable, about a woman with ten coins who loses one and searches thoroughly until she finds it. Finally, there is the well-known story of the so-called prodigal son, whose father celebrates and rejoices when the lost son returns home. These parables illustrate an important aspect of Jesus's ministry that Luke wishes to drive home: Jesus has come for all, especially for those who are lost. He came for sinners, tax collectors, and Gentiles. Luke's inclusion of these stories supports his overall picture of Jesus as one whose love encompasses all.

Luke also includes the story of two disciples on the road to Emmaus, who encounter the resurrected Jesus in Luke 24. They don't recognize him at first, but later recall their hearts "were on fire" as they spoke with him (24:32). They describe to Jesus the events surrounding his crucifixion, at which point Jesus teaches them that everything that happened was foretold by the prophets. "He interpreted for them the things written about himself in all the scriptures, starting with Moses and going through all the prophets" (24:27). Like Matthew, Luke emphasizes the continuity between Jesus and the Old Testament, a theme that continues in Acts, which Luke also wrote.

In Luke 24, Jesus himself is the one who helps the disciples see the Scriptures anew, reading them with fresh eyes in light of Jesus's death and the reports of his resurrection. For Luke, Jesus is the lens through which all of Scripture and tradition must now be interpreted, even as these same Scriptures guide us in understanding that Jesus was God's Son and the Christ. Luke wrote his whole Gospel with this understanding, crafting it in a way that draws out the deep resonances between Jesus's life, death, and resurrection and the story of God's people recounted in the Old Testament.

DAY 278

Luke 15:1–16:31

Luke 15 reminds us that God loves finding lost things: a sheep, a coin, a prodigal son…and us. It's followed by Luke 16, which is about wealth: gaining it dishonestly, flaunting it, and not sharing it. Luke 15 tells us we have been found by grace; Luke 16 tells us we should respond to that grace with a faithful use of our finances.

DAY 279

Luke 17:1–18:43

Luke 17–18 reminds us of what it means to follow Jesus: forgiveness, gratitude, persistence, humility, generosity, and faith. It is a good list to aim for every day.

DAY 280 *Luke 19:1-48*

Luke 19 begins with Zacchaeus, who welcomed Jesus into his house and then decided to give half his money to the poor. It ends with Jesus cleaning God's house of those who monetized the Temple for personal gain. Jesus is serious about our relationship with wealth.

DAY 281 *Luke 20:1–21:38*

It's always important to remember that Jesus's greatest rebukes were not at people who were irreligious nonbelievers, but against religious people who were hypocritical, dogmatic, and who cared little for the oppressed. In what ways are we like that?

DAY 282

Luke 22:1-71

The disciples who shared in Jesus's last meal included Judas who would betray him, Peter who was blind to his pride, and the rest who fought for power. Jesus doesn't pick perfect people to follow him, but calls us to learn how to follow him faithfully.

DAY 283

Luke 23:1-56

The Gospel that opens by elevating the role of women also emphasizes the role that women played at the end of Jesus's life. Jesus blesses the barren, and Luke tells us women were with him until the end and prepared him for burial. In what ways can we be more honoring of women?

DAY 284   *Luke 24:1-53*

It's no accident that the disciples on the road to Emmaus did not recognize the Resurrection until they ate together with Jesus. It's why an open table is important: everyone is invited to experience new life in Christ for themselves.

NOTES & REFLECTIONS

John 1:1–10:42

By the time we get through Luke's Gospel, we might think we've heard all there is to hear about Jesus. Good things usually come in threes, so they say, so after reading Matthew, Mark, and Luke, we might think there is nothing important left to hear. Three accounts of the Resurrection, three versions of the feeding of the multitude, two versions of the birth of Jesus. Not to mention all the parables, all the miracles, all the teachings. We get it.

And then along comes John's Gospel. Written decades after the other three, and the writer not only tells us there is more to say, he is interested in telling us about Jesus in a very different way altogether.

That's what John's Gospel is. It's not a sequel, it's not a prequel, and it's not a replay. It is a reboot of the Jesus story, telling us about Jesus in a way that is consistent with the other Gospels, but doing so in a way that emphasizes different things, capturing different aspects of who Jesus is and why his life, death, and resurrection are important.

Some of the most treasured and widely known biblical passages of all time come from John's Gospel. "God so loved the world that he gave his only Son, so that everyone who believes in him won't perish, but will have eternal life." That's in John's Gospel, chapter 3, verse 16. "I am the way, the truth and the life. No one comes to the Father except through me." That's in John's Gospel, too (14:6). So is this: "I came so that they could have life—indeed, so that they could live life to the fullest" (10:10).

The theme verse for John's Gospel is found in chapter 20, verse 31: "But these things are written so that you will believe that Jesus is the Christ, God's Son, and that believing, you will have life in his name." John tells the story so that you, reader, may come to believe that Jesus is the Messiah, the Son of God.

The word *believe* is used in John's Gospel more than any in another book in the Bible. John knows that choosing to believe in Jesus is the single most important choice that a person can make. Because when a person chooses to believe in Jesus, she or he receives not just a life, but an abundant life, a re-created life.

Time and time again, Jesus will have personal, private encounters with people who are confronted by the question of whether to believe in Jesus or not. In fact, there are more private, one-on-one encounters between Jesus and individual persons in John's Gospel than in any of the other three Gospels combined. Jesus and Nicodemus. Jesus and the Samaritan woman at the well. Jesus and Martha after Lazarus's death. Jesus and Pilate on Good Friday. Jesus and Mary at the empty tomb. Jesus and Peter at the very end of the Gospel.

And John would turn the focus on you, so that you might find yourself in this Gospel, in a private, personal conversation with Jesus, and ask you the question: Do you believe in Jesus or not? Because if you do, you will discover life, fuller and more abundant than you can ever imagine.

DAY 285

John 1:1–2:12

John 1 is a reboot of Genesis 1: both open with "In the beginning." God spoke creation into being. ("The Word was with God / the Word was God," v. 1) God said let there be light. ("Through the Word was life, / and the life was the light for all people," v. 4.) God separated the waters. (Jesus's first sign involved transforming water.) We can be part of God's new creation in the world today.

DAY 286

John 2:13–3:36

The most famous verse in the New Testament (John 3:16) is a response to a man questioning Jesus in the dark (3:2), which itself was a response to Jesus upsetting conventional wisdom (2:13-16). Darkness and doubt aren't fun, but they can be the gateways to new understanding.

DAY 287

John 4:1-54

In John 4, Jesus was physically tired, thirsty, and hungry. But his deeper hunger was satisfied when he shared the good news with someone who was spiritually searching (v. 34). Physical food satisfies for a short while. Spiritual food impacts eternity.

DAY 288

John 5:1–6:21

John 5–6 has two water miracles: the healing of the paralyzed man by the pool, and the walking on water. In between is the feeding of the five thousand with a boy's offering. All these stories remind us of the power of baptism and Communion, and that Jesus is always present among us.

DAY 289

John 6:22–7:9

John 6:26-27 is a key passage. We must not make following Jesus about meeting our needs. Worship is not about entertaining us, prayer is not about blessing us, Bible reading is not about feeding us. It's about what we surrender, offer to Jesus, and believe.

DAY 290

John 7:10–8:59

People are divided about Jesus: Those who believe or don't believe; those who want him arrested or those who are amazed; those who question his authority or those set free by his truth. In John, it's a binary choice: Are you with or against Jesus?

DAY 291

Caught in the crosshairs of the squabbling by the Pharisees is a man born blind whom Jesus healed in John 9:13-34. By the end of the story, it's the Pharisees who are the truly blind, and those who believe in Jesus now can see. Which group do you identify with more?

NOTES & REFLECTIONS

John 11:1–Acts 5:16

In this week's readings we conclude the Gospel of John and begin the Book of Acts.

One of the distinguishing features of John is the "I am" statements of Jesus. Seven times in this Gospel, Jesus describes himself with a statement that begins with the words, "I am." It's a nod to the way God's name was revealed to Moses in the Book of Exodus. When Moses asked God's name, God told him "I Am Who I Am" (Exodus 3:14).

These seven "I am" statements are John's way of telling the world that Jesus is God. Just to prove it, Jesus not only says he is God, he demonstrates it. And each time, there is an invitation to recognize that we are not God. We must look to Jesus for salvation, not ourselves.

When Jesus says, "I am the bread of life" in John 6 (v. 35), he couples it with the feeding of bread to a hungry crowd. Jesus is the bread of life, and that means we are not. We cannot feed ourselves the kind of spiritual nourishment that only God can provide.

When Jesus says, "I am the light of the world" in John 8 (v. 12), he couples it with the healing of a blind man. Jesus is the light, and that means we are not. There is no hidden light within us that we need to discover in order to see spiritual things clearly.

When Jesus says, "I am the gate" and "I am the good shepherd" in John 10 (vv. 7, 11), he compared his disciples to the sheep who hear his voice and worldly leaders to those who would steal them away. Jesus is the gate and the good shepherd, and that means that we are not. We cannot secure for ourselves the kind of peace, security, and comfort that only God can provide.

When Jesus says, "I am the resurrection and the life" in John 11 (v. 25), he couples it with the raising of Lazarus from the dead. Jesus is the

Resurrection, and that means we are not. We cannot resurrect ourselves from the dead. We cannot bring new life from deep within us.

When Jesus says, "I am the way, the truth, and the life" in John 14 (v. 6), he is about to walk the way toward the cross on Golgotha. Jesus is the way, and that means we are not. As much as we feel compelled to find our way in life, in our profession, and in our future, the only way to find true life is in Jesus, not within us.

When Jesus says in John 15 (v. 1), "I am the true vine," he describes not only himself, but you and me as well. "I am the vine; you are the branches," Jesus says (v. 5). Jesus opens a window into ourselves, and invites us to see something within us that we may have never noticed before. It is the branches that bear fruit. To produce the figs, grapes, olives, that will not only nourish others, but will create beauty, and propagate the species.

You have the ability to bear fruit for Jesus. You are designed to offer God's goodness, and beauty, and love for the world. It is what you are wired to do. We are not the vine. We can't do it without Jesus. We cannot save ourselves, much less save the world. "Without me," Jesus says, "you can't do anything" (v. 5). But with Jesus, we can offer the world the kind of hope, and joy, and love that it so desperately needs right now.

DAY 292 *John 11:1–12:50*

Jesus spends much of John 11 telling people that Lazarus's death won't be permanent. Yet, when a grieving Mary tells him Lazarus is dead, Jesus weeps. Why? Not because he believed death won. But so that in Jesus, we have someone who grieves with us. Even after Lazarus was raised from the dead, he still needed to be unbound. Even though we receive new life in Christ, we still need to be daily unbound from our old ways.

DAY 293 *John 13:1–14:31*

Feeling unloved or incapable of receiving or sharing love? Read John 13–14. Jesus's last night with the disciples reminded them to love, showed them how to love, and prayed the Spirit's love upon them. And it begins with John 13:1: "He loved them to the end" (NRSV).

DAY 294
John 15:1–17:26

Jesus gives us three key values in John 15–17: love, truth, and unity. All are important. Love without the other two is inconsequential sentiment. Truth alone can lead to dogmatism. Unity alone can actually cause harm. The Holy Spirit helps ensure the balance.

DAY 295
John 18:1–19:42

John portrays Pilate in chapters 18–19 as less of a villain and more of a curious seeker. He asked Jesus, "What is truth?" (18:38) because Jesus did not fit into his way of thinking. When Jesus upends our thinking, are we open to him, or do we wash our hands of him?

DAY 296 *John 20:1–21:25*

John begins with such a high view of Jesus (John 1) yet ends with an intimate view of how he relates to us. He connects to us personally (Mary, Peter), he had scars (Thomas), and he ate with his friends (fish). And John's Gospel ends with a command to be the same for others ("Feed my sheep").

DAY 297 *Acts 1:1–2:47*

Pentecost is a glorious day of the church year. It hasn't (yet) been touched by commercialism, and the same Holy Spirit that appeared to the disciples that day is the same Spirit we can experience today. It is our entry point in the Bible. It is now our story.

DAY 298

Acts 3:1–5:16

Acts 3–5 reveals these important truths about God. God can heal, God cannot be silenced, God can empower us to share with others, God cannot be lied to. Our response should be: be a conduit for God's healing, proclaim God's truth, share God's love, and live with God's integrity.

NOTES & REFLECTIONS

Acts 5:17–23:35

This week's readings continue the Book of Acts, which we began last week. Acts was written by the same author as the Gospel of Luke, and it reads like a continuation of Luke. You'll recall that a defining element of Luke's Gospel is God's expansive, inclusive love for all people. We see that same trajectory in Acts, as the Holy Spirit guides the apostles in proclaiming the good news of Jesus Christ first in Jerusalem, then throughout Judea and Samaria, and finally "to the end of the earth" (1:8).

In fact, we may regard Acts as a pivotal moment in the entire Bible, with Acts as a significant crossroads moment that sets the universal scope of God's story.

The Old Testament story begins with Creation, includes the covenant with Abraham, Isaac, and Jacob, followed by the story of the Exodus and the occupation of the Promised Land, then God's covenant with David. It includes the troubled history of the kings in Israel and Judah, culminating in the Babylonian Exile, the prophetic words of judgment, comfort, and hope to make sense of it all, and eventually the return to Jerusalem and rebuilding of the Temple. Through it all, the central theme is that the Lord is the one true God, Creator of the universe; the Lord is our God; and we are God's people. It starts with the grandeur of the whole creation and reminds us that we have an exclusive relationship with God. We are claimed, we are chosen, and we are called to live in a certain way.

And then comes Jesus, God's Son, and the story shifts. No longer is God understood to have a special relationship with the Israelites only. Belief in Jesus, the choice to follow Jesus by the Holy Spirit, is now the defining characteristic of what it means to be God's people, and this is available to all who believe. The story we read in Luke and Acts is one in which an ever-widening circle of people come to believe in Jesus. The Canaanite woman, the Samaritan woman, the Roman centurion in the

Gospels. Go into the world, Jesus says in Matthew 28, to make disciples of all people. And then we get to Acts, where the message of Jesus and the salvation he brings goes far and wide. In Acts 1, Jesus says that the disciples will be his witnesses in Jerusalem, Judea, Samaria, to the end of the earth. And then Acts 2, with a list of different people and languages who hear and believe the good news at Pentecost. Then comes Peter's vision in Acts 10 and the conversion of Cornelius, where Gentiles receive the Holy Spirit and baptism.

The Old Testament is about being chosen, called, and commanded to live a holy life.

And the New Testament is about receiving, believing, and sharing the love of Jesus with all people, empowered and emboldened by the Holy Spirit.

That's the Bible in a nutshell. That's the story that you and I get to step into.

Acts relates the story of the Holy Spirit, working through the apostles, our ancestors of faith, to bring the love of Jesus and the message of salvation to the end of the earth. As you read it this week, remember that this story is part of our ancestry, and just as it was a defining moment for the history of the church, it can be a defining moment for you, about how you will choose to live, relate to others across our differences, and generously share God's love with the world today.

DAY 299
Acts 5:17–7:60

Acts 5–7 contains a biblical basis for civil disobedience. When the laws of the land, and even of institutional religion, contradict the values and work of God's mission, Peter offers this word: "We must obey God rather than humans!" (5:29).

DAY 300
Acts 8:1–9:43

Acts starts with crowds coming to believe, but shifts to the stories of individuals. In Acts 8–9, each person is transformed because of a friend: Simon (Philip), the eunuch (Philip), Saul (Ananias), Dorcas (Lydia). We are to be that friend for someone else.

DAY 301 *Acts 10:1–12:25*

Three o'clock p.m. is an important time in the Bible. It's when Jesus died, when Paul experienced his dramatic transformation, and when Peter received his vision. Do we take time for God in the middle of the day? Also, the city of Joppa is significant. It's where God called Jonah and where Peter received his vision. On both occasions, God gave Jonah and Peter a wider vision of God's love for all people, not just a select few. What is my "Joppa" moment? Where is God showing me that God includes those whom I would rather exclude?

DAY 302 *Acts 13:1–15:21*

God's love is not proprietary. It does not belong to us, for us to determine who is "in" and who is "out." The circle is wider than we think it is, and it doesn't include just us.

DAY 303   *Acts 15:22–17:34*

Paul shows us what it means to be "evangelical" in the best sense: meeting people where they are, pursuing social justice, speaking the language of the culture, and "turning the world upside down" (17:6 NRSV).

DAY 304   *Acts 18:1–20:38*

Just like the parable of the sower, Paul's efforts had mixed results. Sometimes people were responsive, and other times they rejected him. It is a reminder that we are not called to be successful, but simply to be faithful.

DAY 305

Acts 21:1–23:35

Paul tapped into his Jewishness to speak to Jews, his Roman citizenship to speak to Gentiles, and his legal background to speak to religious officials. We need to be theologically multilingual, sharing Jesus by meeting people where they are.

NOTES & REFLECTIONS

Acts 24:1–Romans 13:14

This week we conclude the Book of Acts and start on the Epistles, beginning with Paul's letter to the Romans. The New Testament contains thirteen Epistles attributed to Paul, though biblical scholars dispute whether all thirteen were written by him. At least seven of them were: Romans, 1 and 2 Corinthians, Galatians, Philippians, 1 Thessalonians, and Philemon.

Romans is the longest of Paul's letters and the first we encounter in the New Testament, though it is not the first one he wrote. Paul's letter to the Romans has been profoundly influential on the Christian faith, as interpreters from St. Augustine to Martin Luther have regarded it as a key to understanding Paul and the Christian faith as a whole. Paul did not found the church in Rome, and he had never visited it at the time he wrote his letter. The letter is, in a way, Paul's introduction of himself to the Roman Christians in advance of his planned visit. In it, Paul writes about the salvation offered to all people through Jesus Christ.

A number of key themes emerge in Paul's letter to the Romans, including: the pervasiveness of human sin; God's merciful response, evidenced in the salvation and reconciliation offered to all people through Jesus Christ; the inclusion of both Jews and Gentiles; how Christ sets us free from sin and death; our death to sin and resurrection with Christ into new life. These themes are not unique to Romans, but characterize Paul's writings elsewhere as well.

Paul frequently refers to the Old Testament as he explains the Christian faith, making use of direct quotation as well as allusion. In doing so, Paul affirms the continuity between the gospel he proclaims and the story of God and the people of Israel. Salvation through Jesus Christ, and the inclusion of Gentiles among the people of God, are not departures from God's designs, but rather a fulfillment of what God had intended all along.

DAY 306

Acts 24:1–26:32

Paul was bounced from trial to trial, getting into trouble for preaching about justice, self-control, and the coming judgment (24:25). And he was accused of "too much learning" (26:24). Would that we would each be found guilty of such things.

DAY 307

Acts 27:1–28:31

The Book of Acts ends with Paul in a torrential storm and shipwreck, and finally in Rome, where he preached to the masses. Then it concludes, open-ended. Perhaps we are the living continuation of the story, making Acts a story for us today.

DAY 308 *Romans 1:1–3:20*

The Book of Romans opens with a sobering indictment of humanity. We are broken, prone to harming each other, and unable to keep moral law on our own. Paul is beginning to build his legal case for why we need Jesus.

DAY 309 *Romans 3:21–5:21*

Romans may be the most important letter Paul ever wrote. So much of Western civilization is based on Greco-Roman thought and ideals, and the case that Romans makes for Jesus is the basis for much of our theology today. Romans 3–6 is the gospel in a nutshell.

DAY 310 *Romans 6:1–8:17*

Romans 6–8 uses enslavement language to explain the gospel. Sin enslaves us, removing our personhood and freedom. Now grace enslaves us, giving us personhood in God and disrupting our freedom to sin. As John Wesley says in the well-known Covenant Prayer, "I am no longer my own, but Thine."

DAY 311 *Romans 8:18–10:21*

God's love is expansive and inclusive. It breaks through every barrier that might separate us from God, and it shows no favoritism to any one people. Our response to God's love then is to claim it and share it.

DAY 312   *Romans 11:1–13:14*

The first two-thirds of Romans is about belief; this last third is about behavior. Romans 12–16 is easier to understand, but harder to apply. We are called to obedience, humility, prayer, peace, and most of all, love. Nothing else but love mattered for Paul, and nothing else should matter for us.

NOTES & REFLECTIONS

Romans 14:1–2 Corinthians 3:18

Paul's letters addressed specific communities of early Christians, and typically they addressed specific circumstances that pertained to those communities. On the one hand, this can make it challenging to see how some of Paul's writings can guide us today; not all of the situations they faced are as urgent or even relevant for Christians in the twenty-first century. On the other hand, Paul's writings give us valuable insight into the early church, the theological and social questions they grappled with, the hardships they faced, and the hope that they held in Christ.

Paul's letters to the Corinthians are excellent examples of Paul writing for a specific audience to address specific situations. The church in Corinth is one that Paul had established, with which he maintained contact as his missionary travels took him elsewhere. From Paul's letters we can see that the church had members from differing social backgrounds, which may have generated conflict. Certain members were taking other members to court, and the Lord's Supper was a source of division rather than of community. There were differing opinions over whether it was allowable to eat meat that had been sacrificed to idols, questions about marriage and divorce, and issues surrounding spiritual gifts. Paul addressed all of these matters in 1 Corinthians, and his response to them offers a window into the life of the early church. His second letter to the Corinthians shows us that Paul himself experienced conflict with the community that he founded.

While some of these matters seem less relevant for us today, others remain urgent in our Christian communities. How can we celebrate one another's spiritual gifts while maintaining that they are given for all and meant to be used to build up the whole body of Christ? How can the church welcome people of all backgrounds and make all feel at home, a part of Christ's body? How can our life together bear witness to the reality of the resurrection of the dead and the hope that we have as a result?

Above all, Paul writes in 1 Corinthians 13, is the need for us to love one another. This is the foundation of our life together as Christians. Without love, our spiritual gifts are received in vain and our conflicts multiply. But if love characterizes our community and our way of life, it is a powerful, eternal force that endures all things.

DAY 313 *Romans 14:1–16:27*

We can't help but imagine what a better country, world, and church we would have if we all took Romans 14 to heart: Pursue peace. Don't judge or live for yourself or let your strong convictions get in the way of your relationships. Could you imagine?

DAY 314 *1 Corinthians 1:1–3:23*

Few churches were as culturally divided as the Corinthians. First Corinthians 1–3 reminds us that no one has cornered the market on ultimate truth, for God's foolishness is wiser than our wisdom. It's not about claiming to know it all, but knowing God who does.

DAY 315

1 Corinthians 4:1–6:20

Paul decries sexual immorality, not because sex itself is sinful, but because infidelity is. It is a recurring theme throughout the Old Testament: faithfulness in marriage is a metaphor for faithfulness to God. Paul goes even further, saying we are God's "temple" (6:19).

DAY 316

1 Corinthians 7:1–9:27

The issues Paul addresses in 1 Corinthians may seem out-of-date today, but his guiding principles are just as applicable now: self- control, respect for others, concern for those who are weaker, and devotion to God. Regardless of the issue, these values apply.

DAY 317 *1 Corinthians 10:1–12:31*

The Christians in Corinth were plagued by a "me first" mentality, creating division and inequality. For Paul this was a spiritual problem, solved by humility, servanthood, and a commitment to doing everything for the glory of God.

DAY 318 *1 Corinthians 13:1–16:24*

First Corinthians ends with a tour de force of the hallmarks of the Christian faith, which we should remember: the centrality of Jesus's resurrection, the promise of eternal life, a call to service, and most of all, a call to love.

DAY 319   *2 Corinthians 1:1–3:18*

It's a very different Paul writing his second letter to the Corinthians. He has suffered greatly with a restless mind. He's now more humble and heartfelt, drawing strength from those he calls the aroma and living letter of Christ.

NOTES & REFLECTIONS

2 Corinthians 4:1–Ephesians 2:22

This week's readings conclude 2 Corinthians and take us through Galatians and the first part of Ephesians. Paul's letter to the Galatians addresses the question of what Gentile believers in Christ must do in order to receive salvation. More specifically, must they be circumcised and follow other aspects of the Law? Paul's audience, the church in Galatia, has been visited by teachers who preach "another gospel" (1:6) or rather, those who "want to change the gospel of Christ" (1:7). These teachers hold that Gentile Christians must follow the Jewish law, including circumcision.

Paul responds by insisting on the sufficiency of Christ for salvation and on faith in Christ as the only thing necessary. "A person isn't made righteous by the works of the Law but rather through the faithfulness of Jesus Christ," he writes. "We ourselves believed in Christ Jesus so that we could be made righteous by the faithfulness of Christ and not by the works of the Law—because no one will be made righteous by the works of the Law" (2:16). He goes on to contrast the presence and power of the Holy Spirit with human efforts, reminding the Galatians that they received the Spirit through belief, not through their works.

In making his case to the Galatians, Paul tells them he was called by Christ to preach the gospel, so that Paul's teaching does not originate with humans but with Christ himself. He affirms the goodness of the Law by describing it as provisional or temporary, a custodian until Christ came. But now, he says, those who belong to Christ are free from the Law, so now they must live into this freedom, following the Spirit and producing its fruit.

Paul does not say in Galatians that our actions don't matter. Rather, he points to the inability of us by our actions to save ourselves. We can't earn our salvation by following the Law, Paul says, which means we can't jeopardize our salvation by not following the Law. What can jeopardize our salvation is relying on something other than Christ and his faithfulness— and that includes circumcision and other aspects of the Law. Godly actions emerge as the fruit of a Spirit-filled, Christ-transformed life; they are not requirements for us to be a part of the people of Jesus Christ.

DAY 320   *2 Corinthians 4:1–7:16*

Twice Paul again recalls the suffering and hardship he experienced since his last letter to the Corinthians. What kept Paul going? Faith in Christ and love from others, who open their hearts "wide open" to him (6:11-13). We should do the same.

DAY 321   *2 Corinthians 8:1–10:18*

So-called prosperity gospel preachers have warped 2 Corinthians 9 to suggest that if you give money to the church, God will make you rich. Not at all. Rather, Paul is saying that God already has everything necessary to transform the world. It's just up to us to surrender it.

DAY 322   *2 Corinthians 11:1–13:13*

Paul concludes 2 Corinthians with a reprise of his sufferings. Yet he offers his greatest encouragement in the whole letter. God told him, "My grace is enough for you, because power is made perfect in weakness" (12:9). Words to live by, especially in tough times.

DAY 323   *Galatians 1:1–2:21*

Paul opens several of his letters by addressing the recipients in a way that highlights their special relationship with God. But he doesn't open Galatians this way. Paul chastises them for veering away from the gospel. In chapter 2, we discover why: the Galatians are not welcoming of Gentiles. Paul's gospel welcomes all.

DAY 324

Galatians 3:1–4:31

The hits continue. Paul calls the Galatians "irrational" because they refuse to welcome Gentiles. He says such actions are done by those who are enslaved to the law. But in chapters 3–4, he makes it clear: You're better than this. Act like it. Welcome all.

DAY 325

Galatians 5:1–6:18

Galatians 5–6 is pretty direct: Don't bite other people. Instead, love them, don't envy, bear their burdens, and work for the common good. Just imagine what a better world we would have if everyone did these things for each other.

DAY 326   *Ephesians 1:1–2:22*

Ephesians 1 has the odd distinction of containing Paul's longest sentences. They are long sets of run-on sentences, as if you were transcribing a fast-talking person with something exciting to say. This is what has made Paul so excited: we have received the gift of Jesus and the gift of praising God.

NOTES & REFLECTIONS

Ephesians 3:1–1 Thessalonians 3:13

When Paul was writing to the church in Ephesus, he was encountering a community that needed healing. They were torn apart by bitter divisions fought over culture wars between Jews and Gentiles. There were Christians who believed that following Jesus meant observing Jewish laws, and there were Gentile Christians who believed that those things were not important. This was a community that was living by a single story that reinforced the idea that they were too different to get along. Whether they realized it or not, they needed a new story to live by.

And that's what Paul decides to give the church in Ephesus. Right at the beginning of his letter in chapter 1, he tells them a story.

Paul tells the Ephesians a story about God and humanity. There once was a time when humanity was far apart from God, in a broken relationship. But God sent Jesus, who welcomed us into a new relationship, in which all the old barriers that separated us from God were torn down, and we had a new relationship with God. Paul basically took the old story that the Ephesians were telling themselves, which was contaminating them, separating them into warring camps, and replaced it with a redemption story in which God took something bad and turned it into something good.

And Paul poses a question to the Ephesians: Which story will you live by? Which story will you allow to define you and shape your actions as a church?

He says, in Ephesians 1, "Pray that the eyes of your heart will have enough light to see what is the hope of God's call, what is the richness of God's glorious inheritance among believers, and what is the overwhelming greatness of God's power that is working among us believers" (vv. 18-19). In other words, look folks, choose to live by the redemption story. And let that define who you are.

But Paul goes one step further and tells them one more thing: if you want to make this story your own, you have got to offer yourself fully to God for the work of the church. The Ephesians needed to remember that they each had a role to play in creating a new narrative for this community of faith. They were one body in one Spirit, called to the one hope of their calling. One Lord, one faith, one baptism. And then, Paul says, each of you are called in unique ways to step into this new story. Some of you are apostles, some prophets, some evangelists. The same is true for us in the church today: some of us are pastors, some laity, some volunteers, some committee members, some new in the faith, some stretching their faith, some longtime members who are discipling others. Each person with a role to play, "to equip God's people for the work of serving and building up the body of Christ" (4:12).

Paul is telling the Ephesians a new story of who they are. They are reconciled to God and to one another. They are benefactors. They are givers. They are called and equipped to serve out of their spiritual gifts. And if they choose to live by that story, a story of redemption, they will rise above their differences and make an incredible impact on the world.

Paul tells us that same story today about who we are as a church. We are reconciled to God and to one another, and God has richly blessed us with amazing ministry and incredible generosity.

DAY 327

Ephesians 3:1–4:32

God's love is without boundaries so that God's people can love without boundaries. Christian unity and mutual respect is a reflection of God's love, so put away sinful anger and malicious talk.

DAY 328

Ephesians 5:1–6:24

It's unfortunate that Ephesians 5 has been used to enforce the subjugation of women. Before 5:22, we read 5:21. It is not that husbands have more authority than women. All of us must be subject to each other. This is about mutuality, not hierarchy.

DAY 329 *Philippians 1:1–2:30*

Philippians 1–2 shows us how to be joyful amid hardship. God isn't finished with us yet. We have the support of others. The way down (humility) is the way up. God is at work in us. We can be lights in a dark world.

DAY 330 *Philippians 3:1–4:23*

Philippians 3–4 contains some of the most beautiful and encouraging words Paul ever wrote. They remind us to keep Christ first, press forward in faith, stay joyful, don't worry, accept God's peace, keep your mind set on God, and receive God's strength.

DAY 331　　*Colossians 1:1–2:23*

Colossians begins with the equivalent of a satellite image of the Christian faith. It is the highest view of Christ in any of Paul's letters, emphasizing Jesus as Lord of the cosmos. But then it shifts to an indictment of false teachers, who get caught up in squabbling over petty matters. This is what a high view of Jesus can bring us: a realization of just how small our view of God really is, along with our staunch, rigid defense of our own perspective. These are simply "human commandments and teachings" (2:22), with no eternal benefit.

DAY 332　　*Colossians 3:1–4:18*

Colossians 3:1-17 is worth reading, rereading, and most of all, applying. It depicts life just as God intends you to live, in which Christ shines through you and dwells richly in you. Imagine the difference that would make in you.

DAY 333   *1 Thessalonians 1:1–3:13*

First Thessalonians 1–3 tells us why Paul shared the gospel with others. Not to amass converts for numbers' sake, but out of genuine love. In 2:8 he says he cared for them so much that he not only wanted to share the gospel with them but also his own life with them, because "we cared for you so much." The question we should ask is not Who needs Jesus? but Whom should I love with my own life? The answer, always, is everyone.

NOTES & REFLECTIONS

1 Thessalonians 4:1–Titus 3:15

This week's readings include several Epistles: the end of 1 Thessalonians, 2 Thessalonians, 1 and 2 Timothy, and Titus. Though all of these letters are attributed to Paul, it is only 1 Thessalonians that most New Testament scholars confidently agree was written by Paul. The others exhibit vocabulary, theological emphases, and thematic characteristics that differ from Paul's other letters.

Of these, 2 Thessalonians is the most likely to have been written by Paul. Scholars who argue that Paul was the author point to differences in time and setting to account for the differences between it and Paul's other letters. In this letter, the author addresses the belief or worry among some that the day of the Lord, that is, Christ's return, has already occurred. He reassures them that it has not yet happened and that signs will precede it. In the meantime, they should be encouraged and continue living with faithfulness and discipline.

The letters of 1 and 2 Timothy and Titus are often called the Pastoral Epistles, since they address such topics as how to lead the Christian community, how individual members and the church should conduct themselves, and encouragement for leaders who have been given a specific commission. They are written to individual leaders, Timothy and Titus, rather than the entire church in a given city. Timothy had been sent to Ephesus to deal with problems caused by false teaching. First and Second Timothy contain reminders of true teaching in contrast to the false teaching that Timothy will encounter, as well as words of encouragement for the leader.

Titus is written on the island of Crete to Titus, who has been left there "to organize whatever needs to be done and to appoint elders in each city" (1:5). The writer gives instructions about what to look for in elders, how to deal with false teachers and correct those who have been misled by them, and how individual Christians should behave in a godly manner. Titus is encouraged both to teach what is good and to do good, allowing his own conduct to be an example of the Christian life.

DAY 334   *1 Thessalonians 4:1–5:28*

First Thessalonians 4–5 is the basis for much speculation about the return of Jesus. But Paul is less interested in how or when Jesus returns, and more interested in our living out the faith every day and not losing heart. It has been used to talk about the return of Jesus in an effort to, in a colloquial term, "scare the hell out of people." But Paul reminds us here that it's better to love the hell out of them instead.

DAY 335   *2 Thessalonians 1:1–3:18*

In 2 Thessalonians, there's something worse than working without observing Sabbath. It's working without actually accomplishing anything of value. Paul called this "idleness" in some Bible translations. Another calls it an "undisciplined life (3:6). It's worth asking: "Does what I'm doing create value, for God and others?"

DAY 336   *1 Timothy 1:1–3:16*

In 1 Timothy 2, Paul says women should be silent in church and are redeemed only through childbearing. Today many (sadly, not all) Christians appropriately deem that command anachronistic. Doing so does not undermine the Bible's authority. It is a reminder that biblical interpretation is inexact and requires trust in the Spirit's work in a particular time and context.

DAY 337   *1 Timothy 4:1–6:21*

Of the many items on your to-do list today, 1 Timothy 6:11-12 may have the best ones: "Pursue righteousness, holy living, faithfulness, love, endurance, and gentleness. Compete in the good fight of faith. Grab hold of eternal life." Check those off your list every day!

DAY 338   *2 Timothy 1:1–2:26*

The second letter to Timothy reveals a different Paul and Timothy: they are more battered and worn by life and ministry. So Paul calls Timothy to remember that God put a gift in him that has never gone away, and it is time to "wake up that fiery beast," so to speak. In times of weariness, we would do well to remember 1:7: "God didn't give us a spirit that is timid but one that is powerful, loving, and self-controlled."

DAY 339   *2 Timothy 3:1–4:22*

The responsibilities involved in being a Christian, particularly a leader in the church, can often feel too big, almost impossible. Paul and Timothy certainly felt that. But press on, regardless of whether the times are "convenient or inconvenient" (4:2). God will strengthen and rescue us.

DAY 340 *Titus 1:1–3:15*

Setting aside the troubling commands for slaves to submit to their masters and wives to submit to their husbands, the overall message of Titus is that character matters. Self-control, sound judgment, and trustworthiness must supersede unprofitable quarrels.

NOTES & REFLECTIONS

Philemon–James 2:26

In this week's readings, we encounter the short letter of Paul to Philemon and make our way through the Book of Hebrews. Philemon is one of the seven undisputed Epistles of Paul—that is, virtually all New Testament scholars agree that Paul wrote it. It's Paul's shortest Letter in the New Testament, written to Philemon about his slave, Onesimus. Onesimus has been separated from Philemon for some reason that the letter doesn't state and has come to know Paul. In meeting Paul, Onesimus has become a Christian, and Paul appeals to Philemon to receive him well, treating him as a dearly loved brother in Christ. The letter doesn't address slavery as a larger issue in society, but simply appeals to Philemon through love to treat Onesimus with kindness and compassion.

The Book of Hebrews is contained among the New Testament Epistles, but its form suggests that it is a sermon rather than a letter. It ends with greetings, but calls itself a "message of encouragement" (13:22) and begins by launching straight into argument, not with a salutation typical of a letter. The purpose of the sermon is to give its audience confidence in Jesus Christ and his saving work, and to encourage them in their own faithfulness to Christ so that they might endure hardship. The Book of Hebrews makes thorough use of the Old Testament in explaining who Jesus is and how his death and resurrection bring salvation, speaking of him as a great high priest who atones for sin not with the blood of animals, but with his own blood, offered once for all. Some have suggested this points to a Jewish audience (hence the traditional name, Hebrews). A Gentile audience is equally likely, however, since as Christians they would have come to know and study the Hebrew Scriptures as well.

The complex and unique way in which the Book of Hebrews relates Jesus to the Old Testament highlights the importance of seeing Jesus as a continuation of the ongoing story that unfolds in Scripture from the beginning of Genesis. The death and resurrection of Jesus, the arrival of God's Son, is a decisive and new chapter in that story, but it is not a radical departure from everything that has gone before. Rather, it is a fulfillment, as now we can see that the Old Testament prefigured the arrival of Christ. In this way, the author of Hebrews finds a deep, enduring value in the Old Testament Scriptures even as he regards Jesus as the lens through which these Scriptures must now be interpreted.

DAY 341 *Philemon 1-25*

In Philemon, we are reminded of how disruptive God's grace can be. It can unsettle dysfunctional relationships and reset them in love and reconciliation. In what way does your desire to follow Jesus put you at odds with others and the world who don't understand the way of Jesus?

DAY 342 *Hebrews 1:1–3:19*

Hebrews 1–3 poses and answers these questions: Do you want to understand who God is? Look at Jesus. Do you want to know who Jesus is? Read the Scriptures. Do you want to understand the Scriptures? Rely on the Holy Spirit. Do you want to rely on the Spirit? Listen and believe in God.

DAY 343

Hebrews 4:1–6:20

Hebrews 4–6 describes Jesus as our high priest, who reconciles us with God through his dual, human/divine nature. In Jesus, God is transcendent enough to remind us that we are not God and close enough to remind us that we are not alone.

DAY 344

Hebrews 7:1–9:28

Hebrews 7–9 says that Jesus is the high priest whose self-sacrifice fulfilled the sacrificial requirement for our salvation. A modern way to see it is that Jesus's willing subjection to violence exposed and ended the notion of redemptive violence. How will you commit yourself to peace and nonviolence?

DAY 345   *Hebrews 10:1–11:40*

Hebrews 10–11 reminds us that while we are not saved by good works, we are saved for good works. Our salvation in Jesus bears a responsibility: to live with a pure conscience before God and to provoke acts of love for each other (10:22-24).

DAY 346   *Hebrews 12:1–13:25*

If most of Hebrews is about how Jesus offered himself as a sacrifice for us, it ends with how we can live as an offering to God. Hebrews 13 is a worthy daily to-do list for a life well-pleasing to God, and verses 20-21 sum up the whole book.

DAY 347

James 1:1–2:26

James and John go hand in hand, not just as brothers and disciples, but also in the books named after them. John emphasizes belief, and James emphasizes behavior. Both are necessary in the Christian life, and each informs the other. We are not saved by good works, but we are saved for good works. Faith without works is dead, but works done without faith is empty. Today, let's ask ourselves, What will I do to demonstrate my faith and show it in love for others?

NOTES & REFLECTIONS

James 3:1–1 John 5:21

This week's readings take us through the rest of the Book of James, which we began last week, and the Book of 1 John. James is well known in Christian history for its emphasis on faith expressing itself through works. Within the New Testament, James is a balance to Paul's letters that insist faith alone is sufficient. For James, faith is a matter not just of the heart or head, but of the body and one's outward actions. "Even the demons believe," James says, in the sense that they assent to the idea that God is one. How we respond to this idea, with trust that expresses itself in action, is what matters. "Faith without actions has no value at all" (2:19-20).

This week's readings also include 1 John, and the next week's readings take us through 2 and 3 John. It's important to remember that the Epistles of John are meant to be read in tandem with the Gospel of John. We are not certain that they were written by the same John or for the same community, but there are clear thematic and theological resonances across these books. Within the biblical canon, the Gospel of John and the Letters of John are meant to complement each other.

And one of the themes that ties these books together is the importance of love and its relationship to belief. The Gospel of John is about belief and truth—coming to a clarity about who Jesus is and claiming it with certainty. John's Gospel contains the words *truth* and *belief* far more than any other book in the Bible.

The first Epistle of John highlights the importance of love. The letter is only five chapters long, but it contains the word *love* more than any other book in the New Testament.

Keeping in mind that we should read the Epistles and Gospel of John together, what is the relationship between truth and love? How are we to live in the way of both John's Gospel and John's Epistles, in a way that is both truthful and loving?

In *The Wiersbe Bible Commentary: New Testament*, Warren Wiersbe once said, "Truth without love is brutality, but love without truth is hypocrisy" (David C. Cook, 2007, p. 608). In their book *The Meaning of Marriage: Facing the Complexities of Commitment with the Wisdom of God*, Timothy and Kathy Keller put it this way: "Love without truth is sentimentality; it supports and affirms us but keeps us in denial about our flaws. Truth without love is harshness; it gives us information but in such a way that we cannot really hear it" (Penguin, 2011, p. 46). We need both truth and love in our relationships, and that includes our walk with Christ and our relationships with others in the church.

The Epistles of John invite us to hold on to love even as we boldly claim the truth about who Jesus is and what he means for our lives and our world.

DAY 348

James 3:1–5:20

There's so much practical guidance in James. Tame your tongue, resist envy, be humble, pray for others, and help them restore their faith. And it ends with where it began: practice patience amid your suffering, and it will strengthen your heart.

DAY 349

1 Peter 1:1–2:25

First Peter is for those suffering and exiled: Live in hope; the future's bright. Live in holiness; you were bought with a price. Live in harmony; you are building something eternal. Live honorably; others are watching.

DAY 350   *1 Peter 3:1–5:14*

It's important to hold to your convictions and to still live in love and humility with one another. A key to doing that is 1 Peter 3:15: Always be ready to profess your convictions, but do it with "respectful humility."

DAY 351   *2 Peter 1:1–2:22*

God has given you everything you need for "life and godliness" (1:3). Full stop. You've got all the raw material to live life as God intends it, including the free will to choose to do so. Second Peter 1:5-8 shows us how to "make every effort" to do so.

DAY 352

2 Peter 3:1-18

Waiting is hard. Second Peter was written to people getting tired of waiting for God's promises to be fulfilled. It's hard, but God sees the long game. What we see as God's slowness, God sees as deliberateness and intentionality. Be alert. Don't give up.

DAY 353

1 John 1:1–3:24

The Gospel of John and the Epistle of 1 John are two sides of the same coin. The first is about belief, the second is about behavior. The first is about truth, the second is about love. The first is about the light of Jesus, the second is about living in that light. Both are necessary for true life.

DAY 354

1 John 4:1–5:21

Love! It's the essential nature of God, the antidote to fear, and is to characterize our relationships with everyone. We love, because God first loved us.

NOTES & REFLECTIONS

2 John–Revelation 11:19

This week we read the Letters of 2 and 3 John and Jude, and begin the Book of Revelation. Second and Third John are both short, but their vocabulary and theology link them with the themes of 1 John and the Gospel of John.

Jude is a short letter written by Jude, brother of James—and likely the brother of Jesus and leader of the church in Jerusalem for a time. His letter conveys God's judgment on godless people and false teachers and urges his audience to support one another in following Christ.

Many people over the years have viewed Revelation solely as a book that looks ahead, as a future predictor of what will happen at the end of time. But that is not the way most of Christian history has viewed Revelation. Using Revelation to predict a specific date for the end of time, or a specific sequence of events that will unfold before Christ returns, is a relatively modern development in Christian history.

Instead of seeking a literal interpretation of Revelation, or trying to decipher how its symbolism predicts the future in a concrete way, a better approach is to see Revelation as a reminder of the power of imagination, and the ability to envision a future filled with hope, and gain the courage to live into that future right now.

Revelation dates to the end of the first or beginning of the second century AD, and the book relates a vision given to a man named John on the island of Patmos. During this time, many of the early Christians were suffering hardship and pressure from their Greco-Roman counterparts. John's vision, with all of its bizarre imagery and unusual terminology, was written as a way to encourage those Christians to keep the faith and maintain courage in the face of persecution.

The book begins with a vision of Jesus Christ appearing to John, followed by seven messages sent to the churches of Asia Minor (chaps. 2–3). The remainder of the book is a series of visions of God's judgment and punishment on the wicked and the ultimate victory of the lamb—Christ—and those who follow him.

The power of Revelation is that it gives us more than just our own vision of the future, driven by our desires and goals for the church. Revelation is nothing less than God speaking to us through Jesus Christ, giving us God's vision for the future so that it might inspire and sustain our life of faith in the present.

DAY 355

2 John 1-12

The Book of 2 John was written to a female leader of a house church. Our spiritual responsibilities should not just be relegated to Sunday mornings, but must include who we are at home and impact how our families grow in Christ (v. 4).

DAY 356

3 John 1-15

"Dear friend, don't imitate what is bad but what is good" (v. 11). Adopt that as your daily filter, and you will begin to live life as God intends.

DAY 357

Jude 1-25

Don't be immoral, don't follow a perverted version of the faith. Those who do are "waterless clouds" prone to prevailing winds (v. 12). Instead, "keep each other in the love of God" (v. 21), which is a good rule to live by today.

DAY 358

Revelation 1:1–2:29

Everyone has aspects of character and private behavior that we don't want others to see. In these letters to the churches, God first affirms their noble qualities, the ones that are visible to the public, but then also says, "But I have this against you," then also critiques them and names their faltering faith, their worship of other gods, their adherence to false teachers. Hearing the truth about our private lives hurts, but it's necessary if we're to live as God intends.

DAY 359

Revelation 3:1–5:14

Of the seven letters to the churches, it's the one to Laodicea that seems most relevant today. It's for lukewarm Christians who choose a faith of convenience rather than full commitment. What would it mean to you to be fully committed to Christ?

DAY 360

Revelation 6:1–8:5

Revelation 7:9 is a powerful passage. It is an image of the kingdom of God, in which there is no ethnic or socioeconomic division and there is unity of purpose: to praise God. It is a vision of the church that we can work toward today.

DAY 361　　　*Revelation 8:6–11:19*

Before *The Hunger Games* and *Divergent*, Revelation was the original dystopian novel: a vivid vision of a future that we can avoid if we persevere and resist in the present. It is less about what will happen tomorrow, and more about staying faithful today.

NOTES & REFLECTIONS

Revelation 12:1–22:21

This week's readings conclude our journey through the Bible with the second half of Revelation. It's important to remember that Revelation is an apocalypse, an ancient genre of writing in which someone receives a vision and writes it down. The word *apocalypse* in Greek means "revealing" or "unveiling," suggesting that the visionary is seeing behind the everyday world to catch a glimpse of the heavenly, eternal reality that underlies and drives what we experience. The visions of Daniel 7–12 are other biblical examples of apocalyptic literature, as are parts of Ezekiel. There are also non-biblical examples, such as the Book of 1 Enoch.

Apocalypses are full of rich, symbolic language and imagery, and Revelation is no exception. For this reason, we must resist the temptation to read it literally. It's also difficult to follow a specific sequence of events through the whole book, because the visions unfold in cycles. When the seventh seal is opened in Revelation 8, for instance, it does not initiate a new series of events, but takes us back to the beginning to view everything again from a different perspective.

Through Revelation, God says to us that in Christ, our future is secure. God is bringing about a new reality for us, in which former realities with their suffering have passed away. In this new reality God will be very close to us, right in our midst. Our tears will be wiped away, and crying and pain and even death will be no more. God is making all things new.

That's what God is saying to you as you read the Book of Revelation. I know it may be hard to hear it, let alone believe it, but this is why Revelation is written. In Revelation you can read for yourself the promises that God is making to you: "All is done. I am the Alpha and the Omega, the beginning and the end. To the thirsty I will freely give water from the life-giving spring. Those who emerge victorious will inherit these things. I will be their God, and they will be my sons and daughters" (21:6-7).

God says, "Look! I'm making all things new" (21:5). May God make all things new in you, throughout the year to come.

DAY 362
Revelation 12:1–14:20

Revelation 14:12-13 summarizes the whole purpose of the book: to encourage Christians to stay faithful and for the church to endure, so that at the end of one's life, we can know that our labors were not in vain. It's an everyday epitaph.

DAY 363
Revelation 15:1–17:18

The Song of Miriam and Moses is thought to be the oldest piece of scripture in the Bible (Exodus 15:1-21). We come full circle here in Revelation 15:3-4, with the song of Moses and in verse 5–8 the bowls of wrath that echo the ten plagues. The Bible ends with where it begins, with a reminder of God's power to deliver us from captivity, and to make right that which has become wayward and wicked. As we close out another year and look to the one ahead, we would do well to remember that "Great and awe-inspiring are your works, Lord God Almighty" (v. 3).

DAY 364 *Revelation 18:1–20:15*

The final battle! Perhaps we can't help but make some pop-culture connections to Frodo vs. Sauron, Harry vs. Voldemort, and Rey vs. Palpatine. But let's remember: this is not the Bible's final battle. And those who want us to believe that the final battle is coming have it all wrong. The Bible's final battle already happened on the cross, and the empty tomb proclaimed the victor. So Revelation is not about foretelling how the battle will end. It's a reminder of who has already won, and how we need to act like it and stay faithful.

DAY 365 *Revelation 21:1–22:21*

The words of the Bible conclude, but the Word of God in Jesus continues as we live out the hope and promise of Christ in the world. "Come, Lord Jesus," indeed. Amen! And thank you for being on this journey! As you reflect on your journey through the whole Bible, what difference has it made in your life? And what of this journey will you continue, moving forward?

NOTES

NOTES

NOTES

NOTES

NOTES

NOTES

Λ AMPLIFY MEDIA

Enrich your small group experience with weekly videos for _The Bible Year_, available through Amplify Media.

Use **Promo Code BibleYear22** to get
3 months free if you sign up for a 1-year subscription.*
Or call 800-672-1789 to ask about our latest offer.

Amplify Media is a multi-media platform that delivers high quality, searchable content with an emphasis on Wesleyan perspectives for church-wide, group, or individual use on any device at any time. In a world of sometimes overwhelming choices, Amplify gives church leaders media capabilities that are contemporary, relevant, effective and, most importantly, affordable and sustainable.

With Amplify Media you can:

- Provide a reliable source of Christian content through a Wesleyan lens for teaching, training, and inspiration in a customizable library,
- Deliver your own preaching and worship content in a way your congregation knows and appreciates,
- Build your church's capacity to innovate with engaging content and accessible technology,
- Equip your congregation to better understand the Bible and its application, and
- Deepen discipleship beyond the church walls.

**Sign up for Amplify Media at:
https://www.amplifymedia.com/annual-pricing.**
Use **Promo Code BibleYear22** at checkout.*

*Promo code valid from October 1, 2021 through April 30, 2022.
After promo code expires, call 800-672-1789 to ask about our latest offer.